JAMES WATSON

JAMES WATSON

A MEMOIR

1879

And ever honour'd for his worthinesse.
CHAUCER'S KNIGHT.

Appledore Private Press
1879

To
ELLEN BYERLEY WATSON
     her husband's true helpmate
I dedicate
     this insufficient record of his life:

    W. J. LINTON.

New-Haven, U. S. A.
   1879

Whoever rightly advocates the good of some thereby promotes
the good of the whole.

John Woolman

JAMES WATSON

Integer vitæ, scelerisque purus.

MY STORY is not of crowned Emperor or King, nor of any laureled conqueror, the slaughterer of his fellow-men ; it is not of One preëminent, whether in the art of war or the arts of peace. I have to speak of only a plain man, indeed a true servant of Humanity, yet unintroduced by History to Fame, but whom nevertheless I will take as an exemplar of some qualities for which we Englishmen pride ourselves,— wholesomeness and integrity of nature, stedfastness in purpose, firmness of will, indomitable courage, with power of endurance, and self-devotion :— a man whose life displayed at once the healthful sturdiness of the antlered oak, and therewithal such gentlest beauty of disposition as knightliest Sidney had rejoiced to know, and loved. Are such men rare ? I trow not. But this man it was my happiness to know, as friend knows friend.

Concerning him, in some forgotten journal, with the date of March 30, 1833, I find the lines here following : his own writing :—

"TO THE HONOURABLE THE COMMONS OF THE
UNITED KINGDOM OF GREAT-BRITAIN AND IRE-
LAND IN PARLIAMENT ASSEMBLED:—

The Petition of James Watson, of 33, Windmill Street, Finsbury Square, in the County of Middlesex, Bookseller, Printer,
and Publisher, at present unjustly confined in the New Prison, Clerkenwell : —

Showeth, — That your Petitioner is imprisoned in default of
payment of a penalty of £20, having been convicted (under the
60th Geo. III. cap. 9) for selling for one penny a printed paper
called the Poor Man's Guardian, containing "·news, intelligence, and occurrences," not having a four-penny stamp affixed
to it.   Your Petitioner is therefore a debtor to the Crown for
the sum of £20.

"Your Petitioner intreats the consideration of your Honourable House to the very severe punishment inflicted upon your
Petitioner by the magistrates of the Bow Street Police Office,
Sir Frederick Roe and Thomas Halls Esquire, by whom your
Petitioner was summarily convicted in a penalty of £20, and,
in default of payment, subjected to six months imprisonment,
without the intervention of a trial by jury.

"Your Petitioner is the more surprised at this injustice, for
in all previous proceedings for similar offences, on the first
conviction, no individual received, at the utmost, more than
three months imprisonment.

"Your Petitioner also informs your Honourable House, that,
in the honest discharge of his business as a general bookseller,
your Petitioner had exposed, for constant sale, not less than
twenty different periodicals, at the price of one penny : among
others — the Penny Magazine, the Penny Cyclopædia, the Saturday Magazine, the Christian's Magazine, the Working Man's
Friend, &c., some of which pamphlets are under the patronage
of the Lord Chancellor and others of the King's present ministers, and the Bishops of the Church of England, as by Law

established : and for the sale of which weekly papers the publishers and proprietors have never received any molestation ;
though the magistrates have admitted that all these publications equally violate the Act under which your Petitioner has
been convicted, and which demonstrates that it is the opinions
advocated in the Poor Man's Guardian that the Commissioners
of Stamps, and the Government, are anxious to suppress, and
not the protection of the revenue against the loss it is said to
sustain from the circulation of cheap political papers.

"In proof of this statement, your Petitioner begs leave to
point out to your Honourable House, that an information was
laid at Bow Street, against the publishers of the Literary Gaz-
ette, and although the number of the publication then before
the Magistrates contained twenty-one articles of news, the proceedings were quashed, on the plea that no other persons but
the Commissioners of Stamps or their agents could lay inform-
ations against offenders ; since which period the publishers have
proceeded unmolested, and in open violation of the Act, with
the perfect knowledge of the Commissioners of Stamps.

"Your Petitioner claims the attention of your Honourable
House, to the fact of your Petitioner being subjected to the
same treatment in this prison as pickpockets, swindlers, pass-
ers of bad money, committers of rapes and other criminal acts
of a like kind, to the great pain and annoyance of your Petitioner, and in violation of an Act 4th Geo. IV, cap. 64, entitled
'an Act for consolidating and amending the laws relating to
the building, repairing, and *regulating*, of certain Gaols and
Houses of Correction in England and Wales,'— which Act
states that arrangements shall be made to preserve the health,
and improve *the morals of the prisoners*, and in another part
of the same Act of Parliament it is expressly prohibited to class
persons for offences like that of your Petitioner with the aban-
doned characters, and crimes before mentioned.

"Your Petitioner has a separate sleeping-cell, of small di-
mensions, usually appropriated to the solitary confinement of

refractory prisoners; to which cell your Petitioner occasionally resorted during the day, to write a note, or read a book, and to escape from the mental torment of hearing from his associates the most horrid swearing and the grossest licentiousness. Yet even this self-inflicted solitude has been denied your Petitioner, by one of the visiting magistrates of the prison, named Samuel Hoare, banker, of Lombard Street, he having strictly prohibited all access to the cell during the day.

"Your Petitioner having to intermix with so many prisoners, the number in the ward varying from 20 to 60, is in constant dread of contracting disease or of being infested with vermin. Your Petitioner is also constantly exposed to the severity of the weather, there being but one fire for the use of all the prisoners confined in the ward. Your Petitioner has complained to the visiting magistrates of the cruel treatment to which he is subjected, but without obtaining any redress.

"Your Petitioner, therefore, appeals to your Honourable House to institute an inquiry into these complaints and to redress the abuses which subject him to the treatment of a criminal; or to take such steps as your Honourable House, in its wisdom, may consider best to cause the immediate discharge of your Petitioner from his cruel and unmerited imprisonment.

"And your Petitioner will ever pray."

To which, before going farther, I would append these Words of a Believer (the Abbé Lamennais): —

When you see a man led to prison, or to punishment, say not in your haste — This is some wicked man who has committed a crime against his fellows!

For peradventure it is a good man who has wished to serve his fellows, and who for that is punished by their oppressors.

The inscription here-beneath is, or not long since was, on the base of a statue erected in 1831 on a little plot of railed-in garden ground, in Burton Crescent, London.

JOHN CARTWRIGHT

born 28th. Sept. 1740; died 23d. Sept. 1824:

THE FIRM, CONSISTENT, AND PERSEVERING ADVOCATE
OF UNIVERSAL SUFFRAGE, EQUAL REPRESENTATION,
VOTE BY BALLOT, AND ANNUAL PARLIAMENTS.

It was the eve of the "Reform Bill," passed in 1832 by the Whigs under the leadership of Earl Grey, an ancient professor of Major Cartwright's faith. Not that in office the Party attempted to carry out their earlier principles. Content with a £10 household qualification for electors in boroughs and a leasehold, or a copyhold, qualification for electors in counties, they gave to the middle classes a privileged share in the government of the Country, to the exclusion of the mass of "the people": so enabling the middle classes to dictate laws after the shopkeeper's heart,— to wit, the Poor Law Amendment Act to check "the growing evil of pauperism," and the Repeal of the Corn Laws — for assurance of freër trade in labour.

Nearly two hundred years had passed since the religious and patriotic uprising of the English Puritans, since the day on which a number of "long heavy swords with the initials O. C. on their hilts" arrived at a certain farm house in Huntingdonshire,— nearly two hundred years since the impaneling of the grandest jury the world has known, for the trial of a King. Exactly two hundred

years since Cromwell entered upon his St. Ives farm, to
watch and wait events.   As yet Thomas Carlyle had not
spoken to remind Englishmen what manner of man this
Cromwell was.   Even Godwin had not understood him.
Universal England had forgotten him : or recalled him
only through her established church services, the lustral
commemoration of the Blessed Martyrdom and the more
galling annual thanksgiving for the unhappy Restoration
of The Dissolute,— those two most religious ceremonies
which, as was well remarked by Walter Savage Landor,
had been perfectly satisfactory had each been but transferred to the other occasion.   The race of the Puritans
had passed away.   The occupiers and tillers of the soil
grew loyal on their stint of bread per week ; hand-loom
weavers upon Yorkshire moors had their occasional cut
of the Roast Beef of Old England from cows dying with
dysentery ; and the factory system, that crowning mercy
of the Trader's Reign, had already begun to indicate its
capacity for degrading and deteriorating our mechanics.
From underground, in coal or iron mines, as yet was no
report.   Mankind knew nothing of the women and little
children buried living there.   Priestley's house, in the
very heart of England, Shakspere's own neighbourhood,
had been burned by a Church-and-King mob, Priestley
fleeing for his life to America ; as Paine also, for daring
to assert the Rights of Man.   Peterloo had given proof
that the yeomanry (ignorant farmers and farmers' sons)
could be trusted to ride down insurgent peasants (blood
for bread); and the gentle hanging and disemboweling
of the Cato Street conspirators * (part of the coronation

---

* Conspirators by contrivance of the Government.   The conspiracy was
concocted by a Government Spy.   No uncommon proceeding with mon-
archical governments : and done, it is said, for the sake of example.

ceremonies at the accession of George the fourth) was a fair sample of the tender mercy of the Crown.   In truth the French Revolution with its fierce assertion of human right had thoroughly scared the lords and gentlemen and clergy and all that was pious or respectable in the kingdom ; and woe to him who dared but whisper a hope of political or religious liberty !   Paine spoke, and was expatriated, outlawed, vilified.   Let the serf keep silence ! The infamous Castlereagh Cabinet (Castlereagh committed suicide in *1822*) had stamped the legend of *Tyranny* on our coinage ; and none other might pass current.

> "Corpses are cold in the tomb,
> Stones on the pavement are dumb,
> Abortions are dead in the womb ;
> And their mothers look pale, like the white shore
> Of Albion free no more.
>
> "Her sons are as stones in the way ;
> They are masses of senseless clay ;
> They are trodden and move not away :
> The abortion with which she travaileth
> Is Liberty smitten to death." *

Smitten to death, and even lament forbidden !   Among other devices, to confine the people ·in that ignorance in which is the supposed security for a brutish submission, was a tax of four-pence on every periodical publication wherein political events were chronicled or discussed : or in legal phraseology, — "which contained news, intelligence, or occurrences, or remarks or observations thereupon, or on matters in Church or State."   In days when the cost of a single letter (postage between London and Bristol one shilling) put it beyond the reach of the day-labourer (nine shillings a week "good wages" for a man

* " *Lines written during the execrable Castlereagh Administration*," by Percy Bysshe Shelley.

with a family of nine *) this tax was equivalent to a pro-
hibition : it was so intended. By which means, with the
additional precaution of fore-given security, required of
the printer or publisher, as provision for penalties to be
imposed by the Government for whatsoever writing they
might choose to call offensive, political knowledge was,
so far as governmental wit could devise, confined to the
respectable classes, whose interests were said to consist
with the perpetuation of helotry. Chained (the chain of
the modern slave is hunger), chained and gagged, what
was to be done toward enfranchising the masses ?

By two ways only can Liberty be won : by the sword,
or by the power of the spoken or the written word.

By the sword ?   The well-born, whose fathers fought
with Cromwell, now, lame with gout and their brains all
muddied by thick port, were at the side of tyranny ; and
where, among the perennially clammed, was to be found
an arm fit to wield the flail of the Lord and of Gideon ?
Brought up and stunted in the upas-shadow of a Church
drunken and disreputable, in the words of Cowper —

" a priesthood such as Baal's was of old,"

the untaught albeit repeatedly catechized populace were
the blind tools as well as victims of oppression ; or took
refuge in the passive discontentedness of such aped pur-
itanism as was inaugurated by Wesley, which looked to
heaven for reward of its surly patience and no more had
care or thought for the establishment of God's Laws on

---

* In the agricultural districts. And for mechanics: date March 1833 :—
"WILLIAM CARTER, Journeyman Framework-knitter, of Leicester : his
average labour seventeen hours a day, his earnings nine shillings a week
subject to the following deductions : Frame-rent, 1 s. 3 d. ; Winding, 4 d. ;
Candles, 9 d. ; Needles, 3 d. ; Master's charge on work, 3 d. ; Coals for
the shop, 3 d. ; Seaming, 10 d. ; leaving 5 s. 1 d. for house-rent, fuel, soap
for washing, food, and clothing, for himself, a wife, and five children."

earth.   By the sword?   And where the swordsmen, the
"strong-limbed and godly men who dare"?   The strong
earning rheumatism at the plough, the godliest skulking
in some conventicle, cursing prelacy, but cursing equally
the "infidel" disturber of that "order" in which prelacy
grew rank.   One bravely spoken word had been heard
in England since the Rascal Restoration : he who spoke
it, — I repeat, and will have again to repeat his name —
THOMAS PAINE, has to this day obtained as little grace
or honour from the lips of dissenting presbyters as from
the rounder mouths of priests or popes.   Who else has
been so violently assailed, whose character so villainous-
ly abused?   Church-legal and Dissent have rivaled each
other in slanderous vituperation against the wretch who
would have broken the double chain of clerical and political imposture.   They made his name a bye-word and
a reproach, and set a mark on whosoever was known but
to have read his writings.   Yet men kept those writings
hidden away, as their fathers had kept the first English
Bible.   And read, but were too weak to act.   For the
mass, not only were they weak, but from their souls was
washed out ("by the blood of the Lamb," in the jargon
of the herdsmen) even the wish for rebellion.   Pig-like,
worse than sheepish, they grunted around their troughs,
listened or did not listen to the Te-Deums of the swine-
herds ; and in due season were gathered to their fathers
— in the smoke-room.   Thicker darkness than wrapped
old Egypt plagued by Moses swathed anarchic England
in those days.   A few alone,* like Cartwright, from time

* Among them not to be forgotten Benjamin Flower, the Editor of the
Cambridge Intelligencer, with his profound reverence for womanhood,
the father of two of the most beautiful and most gifted and influential
women in England, — Eliza Flower, the musical composer, and Sarah,
author of *Vivia Perpetua*, *Hymns*, &c. the wife of W. Brydges Adams.

to time ventured to repeat the first principles of government ; and whoso could might read the hand-writing on
the wall : else no glint of light was visible in the gloom
save some sparks of the fire which France had kindled,
scattered by the hand of Paine.   One Richard Carlile
(not Thomas Carlyle nor of his kindred) thought it were
well to keep some heat alive by republication of Paine's
works.   One William Carpenter looked for a chance of
redemption through the mediation of a free and untaxed
press.   Rebels, but not men of war, they believed in the
might of the Word, which sometimes is able to prevent
the Sword ; and hoped, for themselves and their fellows,
to vindicate that first of all liberties, the Miltonic liberty
" to know, to utter, and to argue freely according to con-
science."   Single-handed each began to put his thought
into action.   With them to will was to do.   Give them
honour for so much !   Not all men are so brave.

Of Carlile, on account of his connection with Watson,
there is need to say something more.   Carlile began his
work in the day of a crazy king, a profligate regent, and
a corrupt government, 1817.   The son of a shoe-maker,
he was born in 1790 at Ashburton in Devonshire.   As a
boy he collected faggots to burn in effigy " Tom Paine,"
the " Guy Fawkes " of that time.   Apprenticed to a tin-
plate-worker (Bunyan also was a tin-man), he followed
that business until his twenty-sixth year, when, meeting
with Paine's works, he was converted, and moved to eke
out scant employment by the sale of Cobbett's *Register*,
Wooler's *Black Dwarf*, and other " radical " periodicals
which the authorities were anxious to suppress : none of
which however he thought bold enough.   Some success
as a vendor led him to publish on his own account : first
Paine's political and afterwards his theological writings.

He brought out too Southey's *Wat Tyler*, when the poet turned conservative would have suppressed it, selling of it twenty-five thousand copies; also Hone's *Parodies*, if every one else was afraid to meddle with them: parodies on the Church Services, which cost him eighteen weeks of prison pending the trial of Hone, whose acquittal released him.   Later however, in November 1819, he was sentenced, as a publisher of "blasphemous and seditious libels," to suffer three years imprisonment in Dorchester jail, with a fine of £1500.   In his defence he read to the Court the whole of Paine's *Age of Reason*, and outwitted his preventers by printing the whole in a cheap form as part of the report of the trial — a privileged publication. In February 1821 his wife was imprisoned; and later in the same year his sister also.   Nevertheless the sale of his publications went on, volunteers helping, until it was judged necessary to form a "Constitutional Association" with the name of Arthur Duke of Wellington heading a list of subscribers, to provide funds, to defend State and Church by the vigourous prosecution of Carlile's shopmen and assistants.   Susanna Wright, William Holmes, George Beer, John Barkley, Humphrey Boyle, William Tunbridge, Joseph Rhodes, JAMES WATSON, and others, so prosecuted, suffered terms of imprisonment, from six months to three years.   Some samples of the sentences may as well be given here.

JOSEPH RHODES: for selling a "blasphemous" pamphlet, two years in House of Correction, with hard labour, and sureties for £500, for good behaviour *during life*.

WILLIAM CAMPION: for *Age of Reason*, three years in Newgate, and his own bail in £100 to keep the peace for life.

JOHN CLARKE: for selling Carlile's *Republican*, three years in Newgate, and to give bail for good conduct during life.

W. V. HOLMES: two years in prison; there told that "if hard labour was not expressed in his sentence, it was implied."

HUMPHREY BOYLE: in prison for five months before his trial, eighteen months afterwards, had a mind, my lord! "that can bear such a sentence with fortitude."

WILLIAM TUNBRIDGE: for Palmer's *Principles of Nature*, in prison for two years, fined £100, "to be imprisoned until the fine be paid."

So dealt the Law with those offenders. But they tired out the "Constitutional Association," and the Law itself began to limp. So much, without more particulars, may suffice to show the conditions of free thought and free speech in that day of "Bible-and-Unicorn" supremacy; to show also the dauntless temper of Carlile, whose full service of incarceration for the public liberties extended to *nine years and four months*. Before his last sentence, anticipating his being punished by a fine, to be paid — if he would pay it at all — only out of the continued sale of his prohibited publications, and that he might also be required to find sureties for future lawful behaviour, he gave in the following deposition :—

"— And deponent saith that, in case the Court should think a penalty necessary, this deponent has no other property from which he can pay a fine than [his] printed books; and from the political business in which this deponent is involved he can not reasonably ask any other persons to become sureties that his future proceedings may not be construed into political offence: not but that this deponent is anxious to live in peace and amity with all men, but that there do exist many political and moral evils which this deponent will through life labour to abate."

Watson's petition to the "Commons" has date of 1833. Twenty-one years later, no fortune made, nor sought — his business was not money-making, but health needing rest, and a bare sufficiency for life to be expected from the continued sale of his publications even in hands less energetic, — his retirement from business gives occasion for friends to gather round him, to express esteem and gratitude, with presentation of some formal address to be kept as a reminder of their appreciation of his worth. Acknowledging the address, he rendered account of his career. I will not interrupt: his own modest words, as reported with some approach to accuracy, will stand for prologue and sufficiently as text for farther speech.

"I was born in an obscure town, Malton in Yorkshire, in the year 1799. Our family consisted of my mother, my sister, and myself; my father having died when I wanted about a fortnight of a year old; so that I had but one parent to do the duty of two, and I am proud to say that duty was performed with all a mother's kindness and devotion. My mother although poor was intelligent, as a proof of which I may state that she was a teacher in one of the Sunday-schools of the town. To my mother I owe my taste for reading and what school education I received. I could read well, write indifferently, and had a very imperfect knowledge of arithmetic. At twelve years of age a clergyman, in whose family my mother had lived before her marriage, and who paid for the last three or four quarters of my schooling, induced my mother to bind me to him as an apprentice for seven years, to learn field labour, work in the garden, clean horses, milk cows, and wait at table: occupations not very favourable to mental development. At that time there were no cheap books, no cheap newspapers or periodicals, no Mechanics' Institutions to facilitate the acquisition of knowledge. The government was then in the hands of the clergy and aristocracy, the people, ignorant and debased, taking no part in politics, except once in seven years, when the elections were scenes of degradation and corruption. During my stay with the clergyman my mother again became a servant in the family, and well do I remember reading by the kitchen fire, during the long winter nights. My favourite books were two folio volumes with illustrations, one a history of Europe, the other a history of England. My interest in those books was intense, and many times I thought, while poring over them, shall I ever see any of the places here described? and I have seen many of those places since, although my position then seemed so unfavourable. At the end of six years my master's wife died and he retired into Nottinghamshire, which caused my indentures to be cancelled. After this I lived with my mother and sister; but, not liking to be a burthen on them, myself and a companion, similarly situated, resolved to quit our native town and seek employment (and some relatives) in Leeds. We succeeded in finding both. I found employment at a drysalter's as warehouseman, and had the charge of a saddle-horse.

"It was in the autumn of 1818 that I first became acquainted with politics and theology. Passing along Briggate one evening, I saw at the corner of Union Court a bill, which stated that the Radical Reformers held their meetings in a room in that court. Curiosity prompted me to go and hear what was going on. I found them reading Wooler's *Black Dwarf*, Carlile's *Republican*, and Cobbett's *Register*. I remembered my mother being in the habit of reading Cobbett's *Register*, and saying she 'wondered people spoke so much against it; she saw nothing bad in it, but she saw a great many good things in it.' After hearing it read in the meeting room, I was of my mother's opinion.

"In that room I first became acquainted with one who became my friend and constant companion: his name was William Driver. His name and my own were spoken of together amongst our friends in the same manner as afterward my name was mentioned with that of my friend Hetherington. From this time until 1822 I was actively engaged with Mr. Brayshaw, Joseph Hartley, Robert Byerley (my wife's father), Humphrey Boyle, Mr. Gill, and a number of other friends, in collecting subscriptions for Mr. Carlile, spreading the liberal and free-thinking literature and, by meetings and discussions, endeavouring to obtain the right of free discussion. In 1821 the Government renewed the prosecutions for blasphemy, and Mr. Carlile (then in Dorchester gaol under a three years' sentence) appealed to the friends in the country to serve in the shop. Humphrey Boyle was the first volunteer from Leeds. He was arrested, tried, and sentenced to eighteen months imprisonment. On the 18th of September 1822 I arrived in London, the second Leeds volunteer. I served in the shop at 5 Water Lane, Fleet Street, until Christmas, when I spent a week with Mr. Carlile in Dorchester gaol. At that time Mrs. Carlile and Mr. Carlile's sister were his fellow-prisoners. We talked over many plans and business arrangements.

"At this time the plan of selling the books by a sort of clockwork, so that the seller was not seen, was in practice. Notwithstanding that precaution, Wm. Tunbridge was arrested, tried, and sentenced to two years imprisonment, and fined £100. In January 1823 Mr. Carlile took a shop in the Strand, No. 201. Mrs. Carlile, having completed her two years imprisonment, resided in the rooms above the shop. Towards the end of February I was arrested for selling a copy of Palmer's *Principles of Nature*, taken to Bow Street and, not able to procure bail in London, was sent to Clerkenwell prison, where I remained six weeks. Two of my Leeds friends, Joseph Hartley and Robert Byerley, then became bail for me. My trial took place on the 23d of April at Hick's Hall, Clerkenwell Green, before Mr. Const and the bench of magistrates. I conducted my own defence. Reports had been circulated that the persons who had been taken from Mr. Carlile's shop were but tools in the hands of others, and incapable of defending themselves: which was not true, as Boyle and others of the shopmen had defended themselves.

"In my defence, I endeavoured to prove from the Bible that Palmer was justified in what he had written, when I was interrupted, and told that I 'might quote from the Bible, but not comment upon it.' I was convicted, and sentenced to twelve months imprisonment in Coldbath-Fields prison, and to find bail for my good behaviour for two years.

"I had for fellow-prisoners Wm. Tunbridge and Mrs. S. Wright. Mr. Tunbridge and I had a room to ourselves. During this twelve-month I read with deep interest and much profit Gibbon's *Decline and Fall of the Roman Empire*, Hume's *History of England*, and other standard works, amongst others Mosheim's *Ecclesiastical History*. The reading of that book would have made me a free-thinker if I had not been one before. I endeavoured to make the best use of the opportunity for study and investigation, and the more I read and learned the more I felt my own deficiency. So the twelve months confinement was not lost upon me. Mr. Tunbridge did not share my studies. The evenings I usually spent with another fellow prisoner (Mr. Humphrey), an intelligent man, who possessed a good collection of books. For three or four hours after dark we read to each other, after which until bedtime we conversed or played a game at cribbage. We found the governor, Mr. Vickery, an old Bow Street officer, a kind-hearted man, more disposed to multiply our comforts than to restrict them. And thus our prison life passed as pleasantly and profitably as was possible under the circumstances. I was liberated on the 24th April 1824, and shortly after visited Malton, to convince my mother and friends that imprisonment had not made me a worse son or a bad citizen. In May 1824 the Government renewed the prosecutions of Mr. Carlile's assistants, by arresting, trying, and convicting Wm. Campion, John Clarke, T. R. Perry, R. Hassell, and several others, some of whom were sentenced to three years imprisonment.

" After visiting Leeds, and the friends there, I returned to London. I applied for employment at a number of places, but found my having been in prison, and shopman to Mr. Carlile, a formidable difficulty, and I incurred in consequence considerable privation. I had however a townsman and schoolfellow in London, whose bed and purse were ever at my service. That friend, I have the pleasure to say, is now present.

B

"In August of this year, Mr. Boyle, who had managed Mr. Carlile's business sometime, withdrew from it, and I was applied to by Mr. Carlile to supply his place. I conducted the business from that time until Mr. Carlile's liberation from Dorchester gaol, in November 1825.

"At the end of 1825 I learned the art of a compositor, in the office in which Mr. Carlile's *Republican* was printed. Whilst there I was attacked by cholera, which terminated in typhus and brain fever. I owe my life to the late Julian Hibbert. He took me from my lodgings to his own house at Kentish Town, nursed me and doctored me for eight weeks, and made a man of me again. After my recovery Mr. Hibbert got a printing press put up in his house, and employed me in composing, under his directions, two volumes, one in Greek, the other in Greek and English. I was thus employed, from the latter part of 1826 to the end of March 1828. In 1825 I was first introduced, by my friend Mr. Thomas Hooper, to the advocates of Mr. Owen's New Views of Society; and to the end of 1829 I was actively engaged, helping to form co-operative associations and societies for political and religious liberty. In April 1828 I undertook the agency of the Co-operative Store at 36 Red Lion Square, and I remained in that employment until Christmas 1829.

"In the beginning of 1830 I visited Leeds, Halifax, Dewsbury, Bradford, Huddersfield, Todmorden, Wakefield, and other places, to advocate the establishment of co-operative associations. In May I took the house 33 Windmill Street, Finsbury Square, and there commenced the business of bookseller. During the excitement occasioned by the French Revolution in July I took an active part in the numerous enthusiastic meetings following that event.

"In 1831 I became a printer and publisher. My friend Julian Hibbert gave me his press and types. The first use I made of them was to print Volney's *Lectures on History*, which I composed and printed with my own hands. At this time I became a member of the National Union of the Working Classes.

"In 1832 the excitement of the people on the subject of the Reform Bill was at its height. The cholera being very bad all over the country, the Government, to please the Agnewites, ordered 'a general fast.' The members of the National Union, to mark their contempt for such an order, determined to have a procession through the streets of London, and afterwards to have a general feast. In April I was arrested, with Messrs. Lovett and Benbow, for advising and leading the procession. We were liberated on bail, tried on the 16th of May, each conducting his own defence, and all acquitted. Towards the end of this year Mr. Hetherington was sentenced to his second six months confinement, in Clerkenwell prison, for the *Poor Man's Guardian*.

"In February 1833 I was summoned to Bow Street for selling a *Poor Man's Guardian*. Before the magistrates I justified my conduct in selling unstamped newspapers. They considered me as bad as my friend Hetherington, and sentenced me to six months in the same Clerkenwell prison. I was liberated on the 29th July, and attended the same day a meeting to commemorate the third anniversary of the French Revolution, in which Mr. Julian Hibbert, the Rev. Robert Taylor, Mr. Hetherington, and others, took part. At the end of this year I was engaged with Mr. Saull, Mr. Prout, Mr. Franks, and Mr. Mordan in fitting up the Hall of Science, in the City Road, as a lecture-room for Rowland Detrosier. In January 1834

occurred the lamented death of Mr. Julian Hibbert. In
his will he again gave me a marked token of his regard,
by a legacy of 450 guineas. With this sum I enlarged
my printing operations. My legacy was soon absorbed
in printing Mirabaud's *System of Nature*, Volney's *Ruins*,
Frances Wright's *Popular Lectures*, Paine's *Works*, and
other. In addition to the legacy, I incurred a debt of
£500 in printing and publishing these. In April I took
part in the great meeting of the Trades' Unions, in Co-
penhagen Fields, in favour of the Dorchester labourers.

"On the 3d of June 1834 I was married. Before a
month was over I was again summoned to Bow Street;
but preferred a short trip to Jersey, where I stayed three
weeks. On the 7th of August the officers again seized
me, and I was taken to Clerkenwell for my third imprisonment. I was liberated on the 21st of January 1835,
and from that time to the present have remained unmolested. In 1836, '37, '38, I was engaged with others in
the formation of Working Men's Associations, and assist-
ted to prepare the document called the People's Charter.
In 1840 took place the trial of Henry Hetherington, for
'blasphemy.' He was convicted and imprisoned. My
friend honoured me by dedicating his trial to me, and I
have been more proud of his testimony and friendship
than of anything I ever received. Since 1841 my book-
selling and public work is known to most of my hearers.

" . . I have trespassed on your forbearance : but I
had one object in view, — to show my fellow-workmen
that the humblest may render effectual aid to the cause
of progress if he bring to the task honest determination
and unfaltering perseverance."

The two great questions to which the life of Watson was
devoted were the right of free speech and free printing
and the right of every man yet unconvicted of disabling
crime to take part in choosing the nation's government.
Or, to speak more exactly, the single question with him
was the elevation of his own class (that of the workman
— the man dependent on his work for daily bread), by
these means : — not without thought of the education to
be obtained even through the struggle for them. Of the
man himself and of what he encountered his own words
have told us. Some additional notice I would give here
of his work : first of what he did for the establishment
of a free Press. I have no complete list; but I find the
following among his publications :—

> Paine's Works, complete. *   [Also issued separately.]
> The Life of Paine.
> "Mirabaud's" System of Nature.
> Palmer's Principles of Nature.
> Volney's Lectures on History; and Ruins of Empires.
> Sir W. Drummond's Preface to the Œdipus Judaicus.
> Byron's Cain; and Vision of Judgment.
> Shelley's Queen Mab, with the prosecuted Notes.
> .   .   Masque of Anarchy.
> Clark's Letters to Dr. Adam Clarke,— on the Life and
>   Miracles of Christ.

* Including the *Address on the Abolition of Royalty*. Translated from
the French, in Brissot's *Patriote Français* of 27 October 1792: unknown
in any previous English version. It first appeared, placarded by Achille
Duchâtelet, on the walls of Paris, on occasion of the King's flight. The
first demand for the Republic.

Robert Owen's Essays on the Formation of Character.
> Lectures; Evils of Existing. State of Society.

Robert Dale Owen: Discussions with Origen Bacheler
> on the Authenticity of the Bible, and on the
> Existence of God.

Frances Wright d'Arusmont's Lectures.

.   .   A Few Days in Athens.

Buonarotti's History of Babeuf's Conspiracy.

Godwin's Political Justice.

Lamennais' Modern Slavery.

Other works, mostly of the English *Index* — marked for expurgation or legal physicking out, not without risk he kept on sale ; but those named above were all, I believe, produced at his own cost, many set up and printed by his own hands, the legacy from Hibbert his only capital. Most of these works were unprofitable : he but asked if a book ought to be read instead of prohibited, would it be useful to his class ; then he calculated how cheaply it could be brought out, content if all his business returns were sufficient for the simplest necessaries of life and to enable him to publish more. The Society for the Diffusion of Useful Knowledge, with harlequin Brougham at their head, and funds and interest without stint, did not show such a list. Their notion of useful knowledge included neither political nor religious, certainly excluded both subjects, except when cooked for the occasion, as were Harriet Martineau's un-truthful Poor-Law Tales. *

* *Poor-Laws and Paupers illustrated*, 1833–4. Harriet Martineau, as it seems to me, has not been quite understood. Instead of being an exact writer, she was in matters of fact most inexact. Her famous Poor-Law Tales, got up to order, to prepare the way for the inhuman Whig "Poor-Law Amendment" Act, are clever romances. She could not wilfully misrepresent, but she gives half-truths, which most often are worse than lies. How much of this was owing to her imperfect hearing, how much rather

And as to social questions — I do not hesitate to assert, the daring of one earnest man did more for the education of the People in those days than all that easy issue of Whig benevolence, all that kindly supply of juiceless chaff for the troughs or mangers of the "insatiable wild beasts," [a parliamentary term for the populace,] whom they hoped so to tame to run more quietly in harness.

In some respects, also, to Watson and to his fellows is owing whatever good came from his rivals: for neither the Diffusion Society's *Penny Magazine* nor its follower, the Christian-promoting *Saturday*, with other "Information for the People" (Chambers'— to wit), had perhaps appeared but for the sake of counteracting the influence of the new cheap literature of Watson and Hetherington, Cleave, Heywood, and others. Like the Whig Political Union (not "national," but only of the middle classes), a new middle-class literature had to be encouraged, opportunity for profit of course duly considered also, lest the malaria from the low lands should infect the healthy dwellers in Respectability, and the comfortable continuance of "Things-as-they-are" be even more influentially vexed by outcries for alteration. So much can the one man win for his age. So much can be done by so little leaven of earnestness.

---

to one-sidedness of brain, it might be hard to say. But the same want of exactitude is noticeable even in a book in which there is barely possibility of personal bias: her *Guide to the Lake Country*, the district in which she lived. Having so to speak of her writings, I am bound also to add my full recognition of the manly integrity of her life; her desire for truth and her stedfast adherence to whatever she thought to be true. She was a feminine Cobbett, sturdy, somewhat antagonistic, honest, well-meaning, but hasty in judgment and expression; notwithstanding all her manliness with the woman's weakness of argument and impulsiveness of assertion.

I have said Watson cared rather than for profit to place
good reading before the uneducated people : wherefore
he was content with the smallest margin of gain enough
for means of life.   But he cared also for the correctness
and decent appearance of his books, even the cheapest.
They were his children (he had none else) : he would
have them well-dressed and fit to be admitted anywhere.
You may tell a man's character by everything he does :
this man's was to be seen in a penny pamphlet.   Good
matter, carefully edited, on fair paper, cleanly printed,
squarely folded, throughly stitched, in plain but always
neat binding or wrapper : you could not but see that it
was done by a consciencious worker, gifted with a keen
sense of fitness and propriety.   He set his face against
the proverb, "cheap and nasty," desiring to break down
the prejudice of his time (not yet quite obsolete) which
confounded radicalism with coarseness and dirt ; sometimes did not lack at least an outer justification.   There
was no mistaking an edition by J. Watson.   To him life
and all its circumstances were to be kept in wholesomeness, though means of beautifying might fail him.   The
pride of the poor man was his.   His honesty should be
clean-skinned and pure, if his clothes were thread-bare ;
his public appearance as his home ever dignified, made
worthy of respect.   Serving in his shop, he had pleasant
and informing words for all who sought his wares ; the
character of this or that book, about which you asked,
might be trusted to his judgment.   His conversation, if
you cared to make acquaintance with it, supplemented
what he sold : what he had given— if apostles in his day
had been able to print and live without debt.   Of debt
he had a horror.   If in his stead [in later days], at the
receipt of custom you found his wife, you could be sure

that he was either at press-work or otherwise employed toward new desired or needed publication, or attending to some public duty—in deputation somewhere, in open meeting, or in prison for his honest, unspared service in the working-man's behalf. In prison he used his leisure for self-instruction : he had no other University experiences. Out of prison he was one to whom the strivers for the Miltonic liberty of speech looked for counsel of sound judgment, and for that certainty whereon to lean which is the prerogative of the most manly— the stay of fibre that can not yield, nor flinch. He was of the stuff [nearly sold out — I hear — a not-paying manufacture] of those old martyrs, who smiled when they were flayed alive, [our modern nerves tremble as we read of agonies they bore] who thrust their hands into fire to pluck out unharmed their more tender souls. For the respect in which his probity and his business qualities were held, his name as treasurer of subscriptions in aid of political sufferers may be voucher enough. He was one to whom you might have trusted untold gold : he *could* not have wronged you of the smallest coin.

I have been able to give some statement of his doings as publisher; of his public work there is neither record nor possibility of adequate recollection. Here confining myself to the endeavour for free publishing, and for the extension of liberal opinions, his books indicate but one direction of his energies. In class meetings, in public meetings, he was as earnest : no man else more earnest. Only his friend Henry Hetherington was more zealous. But Hetherington would neglect his own business rather than the public duty should be left undone. and so was ruined and incurred reproach ; and Watson, wiser, in his home more happily aided, tempered zeal with discretion

and neglected nothing : not even the "mint and anise."
Not the slightest duty unfulfilled marred the perfectness
of his harmonious life.   Yet he,never failed his friend :
and by their side, as prudently active, constant, intrepid,
and devoted, as Watson himself, stood Richard Moore,
to whom and Dobson Collett (the energetic secretary of
the "Society for the abolition of the Taxes upon Knowledge," we mainly owe their ultimate repeal in England,
the remission of that last, worst penny, as it was justly
called, which the shifty Whigs retained when, forced by
the publications and exertions of Hetherington and his
friends to give up their *four-penny* stamp, they hoped by
continuing the lesser but no less offensive hinderance to
be still able to crush the cheap newspapers : beaver-like
biting off what might (but did not) divert the hunters,
to save their miserable lives ; ready ever, as fore-told of
them by Job [or were there Whigs in his time ?] to give
all else, even to their dirty skins.   Am I unjust to these
English Girondists ?   Sir Henry Bulwer answers for me.
"The Whig Party was — always essentially an exclusive
party : *its regards were concentrated on a clique*, to whom
all without it were tools and instruments."   The mantle
of Castlereagh had fallen on them, and they prophesied
in right Tory fashion : Woe to a discontented People !

In the history of the fight for free newspapers — any
record more complete than is room for in this personal
memoir, Hetherington rather than Watson will be recognized as the real leader : Watson himself so placed him.
When, in 1831, the law-administrators declared that any
endeavour to give political knowledge to the people was
ipso facto to be considered illegal, and as such worthy of
punishment, Hetherington came forward to contest their

ruling, by the publication of his *Poor Man's Guardian*, "a weekly paper for the People, established contrary to 'Law' [afterwards published in defiance of "Law"], to try the power of Might against Right: * which will contain [in the words of the prohibitory Act, here in italic] *news, intelligence*, and *occurrences*, and *remarks and observations thereon*, and *on matters in Church and State, tending* decidedly *to excite hatred and contempt of the Government and Constitution* of the tyranny *of this Country as by Law established* and also *to vilify* the ABUSES of *religion;* and will be *printed in the United Kingdom for sale, and published periodically* (every Saturday) *at intervals not exceeding twenty-six days;* and will *not exceed two sheets;* and will be published *for a less sum than six-pence* (to wit, the sum of ONE PENNY); *exclusive of the duty imposed by the* 38 *Geo. III cap.*78 *and* 60 *Geo.III c.* 9, or any other acts whatsoever, and despite the 'laws,' or the will and pleasure, of any tyrant or body of tyrants whatsoever, any thing herein-before or any where else contained to the contrary notwithstanding."

Repeatedly convicted, hunted like a wild beast, imprisoned, stripped of his property, he gallantly maintained the contest to a successful ending: till he forced his opponents to abandon that straining of the Law in which the magistracy had been their handy tool, and to bring him, June the seventeenth, 1834, to fair trial by a jury.

---

* Before this he had brought out daily, and then weekly, *Penny Letters to the People, by the Poor Man's Guardian*, acting upon a suggestion by Carpenter, who proposed so to evade the stringency of Castlereagh's Act. The first of these *Letters* was issued in October 1830; but on his being convicted of illegality he changed the title to the POOR MAN'S GUARDIAN, in bold and open defiance. The first number with this heading is dated 9 July 1831. The *Guardian* was at first edited by Edward Mayhew; and after his untimely death by James Bronterre O'Brien.

The result is told under the heading of the number of the *Guardian* for June 21 :—

"This paper, after sustaining a Government prosecution of three years and a half duration, in which UPWARDS OF FIVE HUNDRED PERSONS * were unjustly imprisoned, and cruelly treated, for vending it, *was on the trial of an ex officio information filed by the Attorney-General against Henry Hetherington, in the Court of Exchequer before Lord Lyndhurst and a special jury, declared to be a strictly legal publication.*"

HETHERINGTON was born in London, in 1792; and brought up as a printer. He was one of the earliest and most active of working-men engaged with Dr. Birkbeck in founding the first Mechanics' Institute; and in 1830 he was chosen by the radical working-men of London to draw up a plan for Trades' Unions, which became the basis of the National Union of the Working Classes, out of which sprang the movement for the People's Charter.

* One of the imprisoned and cruelly treated, as his own story has told us, was Watson. Not in opposition, but in aid of the common cause, he too published a weekly paper, similar to the *Guardian*,— the *Working-Man's Friend*, which escaped prosecution, the fiercer assailant perhaps drawing off the governmental fire.

Among these sufferers for the Liberty of the Press ABEL HEYWOOD is not to be left unnoticed. He was wholesale agent in Manchester for the *Guardian*; and a fair target for prosecution. He took his prison degree; paid his fines when he could afford it; and went on selling his *Guardians*. Then the Authorities seized the papers in the hands of the carriers; and various devices had to be sought, in order that they might pass in safety. Some packed with shoes, some in chests of tea, some otherwise, they sent the proscribed goods through the country; and their circulation continued until the *reduction* of the duty, as was expected, ruined the cheap papers. By this time the *Guardian* had been made the foundation of a business; which Heywood's perseverance and ability enlarged until he, denounced in earlier days as seditious and a blasphemer, became a "well-to-do" citizen, the honoured Mayor of Manchester, and might have sat in Parliament for Manchester had he cared to do so.

For four years he bore the brunt of the battle for a free Press. Ever busy in the interest of his class during the Whig Reform ferment, he was among the most zealous as well as of the wisest leaders of Chartism afterwards. A ready speaker, bold and fluent, passionate, sarcastic, or humourous upon occasion [he had a spice of fun in him through all his trouble], he was deservedly popular in those days ; and in the Chartist Convention of 1839 sat as delegate from Stockport and for London. Time and thought, and toil also, he gave unsparingly in aid of the social and religious striving of the time. He closed his unresting and useful life, after a few days' sickness, on the 24th of August 1849. For his character, I find no better words than some I wrote to be spoken at his burial. There is not a word I would retract or modify.

[Of all the men in the battle for the People's Right, I have known none more single-minded, few so brave, so generous, so gallant as he. He was the most chivalrous of all our party. He could neglect his own interests (which is by no means a virtue, but there is never lack of rebukers for all failings of that kind), but he never did, and never could, neglect his duty to the cause he had embraced, to the principles he had avowed. There was no notoriety-hunting in him : as, indeed, so mean a passion has no place in any true man. And he was of the truest. He would toil in any unnoticeable good work for freedom, in any "forlorn hope," or even, when he saw that justice was with them, for men who were not of his party, as cheerfully and vigorously as most other men will labour for money or fame or respectability. He was a real man, one of that select and "glorious company" of those who are completely in earnest. His principles were not kept in the pocket of a Sunday coat (I don't know that he always had a Sunday change of any sort); but were to him the daily light which led his steps. If strife and

wrath lay in his path, it was seldom from any fault of his: for
though hasty as a man of impulsive nature, and chafed by some
afflictions, he was not intolerant nor quarrelsome nor vindictive.
Men who did not know him have called him violent. He was,
as said before, hasty and impetuous, but utterly without malice;
and he would not have harmed his worst enemy, though, in
truth, he heartily detested tyranny and tyrants. Peace be with
him, on the other side of this fitful dream which we call life:
peace, which he seldom knew here, though his nature was kindly and his hope strong, though he loved Truth and wilfully in-
jured no man. One of the truest and bravest of the warm-
hearted has lain down among the tombs, not worn out, but
sorely wearied. May we rest as honourably, with as few specks
to come between our lives and the grateful recollections of those
who have journeyed with us. If our young men, in the vigour
of their youth, will be but as enthusiastic and as untiring as was
Hetherington even in the last days of his long exertion, we need
not despair of Freedom, nor of a worthy monument to a noble
life, which else would seem but as a vainly-spoken word, wasted
and forgotten.

Yet again, peace be with him; and in his place the copy and
thankful remembrance of the worth we loved in him.]

So much I have had to say of Hetherington, not only
as his due — but too scantily rendered, but also because
for twenty years he was the tried and trusty comrade of
my friend. What Hetherington did was ever seconded
by Watson : what Watson did had surely Hetherington's
endorsement. One can not be praised but the other will
"divide his crown." In Watson's own words, spoken at
his friend's grave, their "single friendship never knew
two interests." During the struggles of the Unstamped
they were as David and Jonathan : the two were as one.
That battle gained, they stood in as close brotherhood
in preparation and in action for the People's Charter.

Hetherington's victory was decisive. The pursuit was left to Moore and Collet. Prosecution was at an end. The logical conclusion required no longer defiance, but persistence only ; and the secretary of the Society for the removal of the yet remaining penny, C. Dobson Collet, might be fitly surnamed the Persistent. And Moore —— I must halt yet somewhile in my memoir of Watson, not to neglect his other friend and comrade, dear to him as Hetherington, yet closer than he, — my own friend also, RICHARD MOORE.

Born in 1810, he was brought up as a wood-carver, in which art he excelled. Early in association with Lovett, Hetherington, and Watson, he shared all their labours ; and marrying a niece of Watson, a wife worthy to be so mated, became yet more intimate with him. For forty years he was among the foremost in all the liberal movements of the time. One of the framers of the People's Charter, he sat in the first Chartist Convention ; he was a leading elector in the radical borough of Finsbury ; he was active in behalf of Poland and of Italy. But most especially he claims remembrance as chairman [Collet, as already said, secretary], during thirteen years, of the Society for the Repeal of the Taxes on Knowledge, the main promoter of that unceasing agitation which forced the Government to give up not only the stamp, but also the taxes on advertisements and paper. Ever labouring with remarkable singleness of purpose in the public service, he was as modest as active. Few men — says one who knew him well —" have enjoyed the confidence and friendship of leading politicians more than he. All the prominent English Radicals and liberal Exiles he could reckon among his friends. . The purity of his life was only equalled by his disinterestedness. . . There was something singularly earnest, gentle, and chivalrous, in his character." . I can only echo these words, knowing how well they were deserved. To him — if the claim of the Wife had not been paramount — this memoir would have been dedicated ; him I had ever in my mind while writing, him first among those for whose approval of my work I cared. True-hearted man and sterling patriot ! no name could be more fitly coupled with your friend's. Only since completing my record of him I learn that in death as in life you are together. Richard Moore died December 7, 1878.

Here too, before I leave the story of the Unstamped, may be fit place to render homage to JULIAN HIBBERT, treasurer, and "chief prop," of the Victim Fund during the battle for the *Guardian*. There is his Life. In his will, out of regard to his relatives, people of "family," his mother (I believe) a catholic, he ordered his papers to be destroyed and forbade his friends to speak of him. "I ask only silence." So passed into oblivion one more of the martyr myriad, the ransom for Humanity. His friends could not but respect his prayer. It is now too late to inquire concerning him. He died in 1834.

His portrait is marvellously like Shelley's. He seems indeed (that I learned) to have been a prose Shelley, with the same gentleness of nature and chivalrous zeal against Wrong ; like Shelley also in his public spirit, in his generosity, his tenderness of disposition, his poetic enthusiasm for what he deemed the Right.

Free publication of honest thought and fair opportunity for sharing in the national government : these two most important of all questions moved, as I have said before, the life of Watson. The second made him a "Chartist." That Chartist phase of English history has been misunderstood or misrepresented by party writers of the time, and seems now almost obliterated from the minds of the present generation of "liberal" politicians, who do not even dream how much they are indebted to it. On this account as well as because of its important influence on the life of England, some words beyond the relation of Watson's actual part in it may not be out of place.

The movement for the "People's Charter," as already told, grew out of a document prepared by Hetherington in 1831, in which originated the *National Union of the Working Classes*, — "to collect and organize a peaceful expression of public opinion," for "protection of working men in the free disposal of their labour," to obtain an "effectual reform in Parliament" (instead of the unfair arrangement projected by the Whigs), "the repeal of all bad laws, and the enactment of a wise and comprehensive code." The association was formed after the model of Wesleyanism : class-leaders being appointed at general meetings to groups of from thirty to forty members, the classes held weekly at members' homes. Those meetings were for political instruction, by readings and discussions. In what records remain of the proceedings I trace Watson's name, not prominent (he never cared

C

to be prominent) but honourably conspicuous. The declaration of principles was drawn up by him and Lovett.

NATIONAL UNION OF THE WORKING CLASSES

" *We, the Working Classes of London*, declare —

" 1 — All property (honestly acquired) to be sacred and inviolable.

" 2 — That all men are born equally free, and have certain natural and inalienable rights.

" 3 — That governments ought to be founded on those rights; and all laws instituted for the *common benefit* in the protection and security of *all the people*: and not for the particular emolument or advantage of any single man, family, or set of men.

" 4 — That all hereditary distinctions of birth are unnatural, and opposed to the equal rights of man; and therefore ought to be abolished.

" 5 — That every man of the age of twenty-one years, of sound mind, and not tainted by crime, has a right, either by himself or his representative, to a free voice in determining the nature of the laws, the necessity for public contributions, the appropriation of them, their amount, mode of assessment, and duration.

" 6 — That in order to secure the unbiassed choice of proper persons for representatives, the mode of voting should be *by ballot*; that intellectual fitness and moral worth, *and not property*, should be the qualification for representatives; and that the duration of Parliament should be but for *one year*.

" 7 — We declare these principles to be essential to our protection as working men, and the only sure guarantees for the securing to us the proceeds of our labour, and that we will never be satisfied with the enactment of any law or laws which do not recognize the rights enumerated in this declaration."

The declaration headed a call for a public meeting of " the useful classes, to be held in the space in front of White-Conduit House, London, on Monday, November

7, 1831, at one o' clock precisely, for the purpose of solemnly ratifying" the above principles.   The Whig Government met this popular challenge by the formation of
a counter association, the "National Political Union"
of the middle classes, to support, by force if necessary,
their class Reform Bill, and to prevent anything beyond
that.   The meeting of the working-men was prohibited
by Lord Melbourne; special constables were mustered;
troops were marched in; and orders were given to arrest
every member of the Committee of the Association who
should appear at the place of meeting.   The temper of
those Reformers — Grey, Russell, Brougham, etc.— may
be sufficiently indicated by this: the Whig Press at that
very time daily threatening the Tories with revolution,
boasting of a hundred and fifty thousand men armed to
enforce their partial measure.   I read in the journals of
same date, of four poor men in Lancashire sentenced,
under an obsolete and forgotten law, to twelve months
imprisonment for *unlawfully assembling on a Sunday evening*.   But they were not assembled for worship of the
Reform Bill.

The Association was wise enough not to accept this
provocation to a conflict undesired and which could but
result in useless bloodshed: it gave up the meeting, and
went on its peaceful way.   In May of the next year a
second attempt at public meeting, preparatory to calling
a National Convention, was put down by actual force:
the police attacked the assembled people.   In the melée
a policeman was killed, stabbed by a man whom he had
struck.   The jury upon the coroner's inquest returned
a verdict of "justifiable homicide," on the ground that
no proclamation forbade the meeting, that the Riot Act
was not read requiring the crowd to disperse, and that

"the conduct of the police was ferocious, brutal and un-provoked." This, at least in intention a fit pendant to the Tory massacre at Peterloo, is what is known as the Calthorpe-Street affair, having happened on some open ground thereby. Care was taken as soon afterwards as possible to build upon the land, effectually to prevent other meetings there.

The National Union did good educational work; but had to give way to the consolidated Trade-Unions, then as now standing, as they always must stand, as obstacles to political endeavour : tempting men with better wages for to-day from what in moments of despondency seems the hopelessness of going to the root of the evil. Still, staunch to their principles, the originators and leaders of the Union made another attempt for the wiser action by the formation in 1836 of the London Working Men's Association,* whose published addresses earned a warm meed of praise, for all his dainty literary taste and care-less poet dislike of political strife, from "the gentlest of the wise," Leigh Hunt. To that association too belongs the honour of sending an Address to the foreigner,† the first public attempt to exorcize the king-fostered spirit of national antagonism.

In February, 1837, the Association, having prepared their way, convened a public meeting at and within the

---

* In a list of those who took most active part in the association I note the names of Henry Hetherington, James Watson, William Lovett, Richard Moore, William Moore, John Cleave, Henry Vincent, Robert Hartwell, Henry Mitchell, William Savage, Charles H. Neesom, Thomas Ireland, S. Calderara, George Julian Harney : names to be ever held in grateful remembrance by English working-men.

† An Address to the Working Classes of Belgium, I believe drawn up by Lovett, on occasion of the imprisonment of one Jacob Katz, for calling a public meeting of workmen to discuss their grievances.

Crown-and-Anchor tavern, in the Strand, (indoor meetings not illegal then), at which a petition to the House
of Commons, for universal suffrage and new ordering of
Parliament, obtained the signatures of three thousand
persons. This petition the Association left in the hands
of Mr. Roebuck for presentation ; and toward his support requested a conference with those members of the
reformed House who professed liberal principles. Eight
came : T. Perronet Thompson, Joseph Hume, Charles
Hindley, Daniel O'Connell, Dr. Bowring, John Temple
Leader, William Sharman Crawford, Benjamin Hawes.
The conference took up two nights, the members of the
Commons' House, except Hawes, assenting generally to
the principles in discussion, but most of them hesitating
as to any immediate promotion of the same. O'Connell
dodged, he would have substituted an ingenious scheme
of his own ; failing which, he agreed with the course of
the Association, — not honestly intending, as afterwards
sufficiently appeared. The following resolutions were
adopted : June 7, 1837.

1 — We agree to support any proposition for Universal Suffrage
made on the Petition emanating from the Working Men's
Association, when presented to the House of Commons by
Mr. Roebuck.

Proposed by Daniel O'Connell.
Seconded by Charles Hindley.

2 — We agree to support and to vote for a Bill, or Bills, to be
brought into the House of Commons, embodying the principles of Universal Suffrage, Equal Representation, Free Selection of Representatives without reference to Property, the
Ballot, and Short Parliaments of fixed duration, the limit not
to exceed three years.

Proposed by Daniel O'Connell.
Seconded by Charles Hindley.

3 — We agree to support and to vote for a Bill, or Bills, to be brought into the House of Commons, for such a reform in the House of Lords as shall render it responsible to the People.

Proposed by Daniel O'Connell.
Seconded by Sharman Crawford.

4 — That a Committee of twelve persons be appointed, to draw up a Bill, or Bills, in a legal form, embodying the principles agreed to, and that they be submitted to another meeting of the liberal members of Parliament and the Working Men's Association: that the following be the persons appointed —

DANIEL O'CONNELL	HY. HETHERINGTON
JOHN ARTHUR ROEBUCK	JOHN CLEAVE
JOHN TEMPLE LEADER	JAMES WATSON
CHARLES HINDLEY	RICHARD MOORE
T. PERRONET THOMPSON	WILLIAM LOVETT
W. SHARMAN CRAWFORD	HENRY VINCENT

Proposed by J. Temple Leader,
Seconded by Robert Hartwell.

The labour of drafting the bill was deputed to Roebuck and Lovett; but, owing to Roebuck's parliamentary and other engagements, fell almost wholly on Lovett. Every clause was carefully considered in the Association, and the bill so completed finally submitted to the public, as The PEOPLE'S CHARTER — "*the outline of an Act* to provide for the just representation of the People of Great Britain and Ireland in the Commons' House of Parliament: embracing the principles of *Universal Suffrage, No Property Qualification* (for Members), *Annual Parliaments, Equal Representation, Payment of Members,* and *Vote by Ballot.*"

On the 6th of August, 1838, at a meeting at New-Hall Hill, Birmingham, the People's Charter was formally approved, even, after some reluctance, by the Household

Suffragists of the Birmingham Political Union. From this time Feargus O'Connor also joined the Chartists. At this meeting it was proposed that a Convention of the Working Classes should be summoned, and a National Petition be obtained, and that a National Rent should be collected to defray the necessary expenses. On the 17th of the following September, another meeting in the Palace Yard, Westminster, the High Bailiff in the chair, solemnly adopted the People's Charter and National Petition and recommended meetings throughout the country to appoint the delegates "to watch over the Charter and Petition when presented to Parliament." At this meeting one of the resolutions was moved by Ebenezer Elliott, "the Corn-Law Rhymer."

The delegates so appointed met, on February the 4th, at the British Coffee House, as the *General Convention of the Working Classes.* The Convention, 55 members, was elected by show of hands of, it was said, three millions of persons: "450,000 had been assembled for the election on Kersal-Moor, 200,000 at Peep-Green, 250,000 at Birmingham, 200,000 at Glasgow, etc." Enthusiasm ran high; money was subscribed; meetings were multiplied; the Convention sent out its members as missionaries through the country; Chartist Associations sprang up in the manufacturing districts, and elsewhere. On the 13th of May, the Convention, having deposited the petition of 1,280,000 persons with Mr. Attwood, transferred their sittings, for the consideration of "ulterior measures," to Birmingham; and then dispersed to hold simultaneous meetings throughout the country. The Petition was presented to the "Commons" on the 14th of June, and on the 12th of July 235 members, against 46, refused to consider its prayer. Meanwhile the Whig

Ministers had not been forgetful of their old tactics, the foolish conduct of some members of the Convention playing into their hands.   Threats of what the people could do were lightly used ; whereupon some sections of them began to arm and train themselves ; ill-founded reports of the war-like determination of the masses were given in to and published by the Convention ; which moreover had neither fore-looking purpose, nor unanimity, nor capacity for guidance.   Arrests were made, for training and drilling ; arrests of members of the Convention for "seditious" speaking.   The Calthorpe Street policy was renewed, and a band of London Police, ordered down to Birmingham, while the Convention was sitting there, attacked the people peaceably meeting in the Bull-Ring. Lovett, the secretary of the Convention, was arrested for signing an address justifying the resistance of the people. And when the Convention met again in London with very reduced numbers, on the 10th of July, it was but to see their Petition mocked at ; to decide, on the 16th of July, upon a "sacred month" — an abstinence from all work for that period, to begin on the 12th of August throughout the country, for the overthrow of the Government ; and to substitute, on the 5th of August, one day's holiday for the impracticable month, and to appeal to the unpolitical Trades, to help a manifestation then. On the 14th of September the Convention dissolved, having utterly failed in everything, except the Petition.

The baseless reports of Chartist power and determination still continued, over-living even the deplorable contradiction furnished by Frost's abortive attempt on Newport, on the 4th of November : an attempt induced by a too-ready credence to bragging exaggerations of others. On the 26th of December a second Convention met in

London, with the object of saving Frost and his fellow-victims. But the game was up. All that remained was the popularity of the ever-active O'Connor and of his *Northern Star*: both of which should have been turned to account.

Lovett, having come out of prison, founded in 1842 the "National Association," to re-commence a general organization. He was joined by most of those who had been most active in the Working Men's Association; and violently opposed by O'Connor and his party, — a party which had been helped by the *Star* to keep up the agitation since 1839, but which had changed Chartism to O'Connorism and almost lost sight of the suffrage while looking for allotments of unprofitable land. But Lovett was impracticable; and his new association, after obtaining a few hundred members, dwindled into a debating club, and their hall became a dancing academy, let occasionally for unobjectionable public meetings. Lukewarmness among the more sensible of the working men, and aimless violence, not without good intention, among the O'Connorites, just kept alive the name of Chartism till the proclamation of the French Republic, in February 1848, awoke old hopes in England.

Then again some efforts were made to resuscitate the movement. Another National Convention met in London, under the auspices of O'Connor, to superintend another Petition. Almost every fault of the first Convention was repeated. Blustering talk led to foolish riots. The Petition with "5,700,000 signatures," afterwards reduced to 2,000,000, including fictitious, was presented on the 10th of April; and on the 17th the Convention dissolved to meet again on the 1st of May, as a "National Assembly," to carry the Charter. But all was now confusion. Even the elections (by show of hands) without principle or method: 3000 men electing three members for London, 100,000 at Halifax electing one. The Assembly simply exhibited its incapacity, and merged into the "National Charter Association," which pursued the same course: gathering tumultous crowds of purposeless men, doing little to teach, and nothing to organize, unable even to command regular subscriptions, and mustering throughout the country only some 5000 paying members after the ten years' turmoil. Those of the Chartists still anxious in 1848, to make some attempt at organization found themselves joined by but a few hundreds, by them feebly, and for a little while. Men no longer rallied around the Chartist banner: some few only when it was dragged in the dirt. Chartism went down in the whirlpool of its own folly.

So much of the history of Chartism I wrote in 1851,* not sparing censure, having to warn the people against a repetition of their folly: for in that hour a few were looking beyond the twilight dimness of a parliamentary reform for the day-star of the Republic. Nevertheless,

---

* *English Republic*, Vol. 1, Art. *Chartism*. In the same article I wrote — From first to last Chartism never had a real intention, that is a clear resolve *to act*; and consequently never made even an endeavour at such an organization as would be necessary for successful action. There was in the National Union of the Working Classes, and elsewhere, ordering for mutual instruction; there were not unfrequent efforts to broadcast political knowledge among the masses; there were well-tried arrangements for getting together so many thousand throats to bawl — "The Charter! and no surrender!" but there never was any serious endeavour to create and weld together a popular power with a determined object, determined means for obtaining it, and determination to act accordingly at whatever risk. The elements of success were left out of view. Nothing else.

History, giving the meaning of Chartism, will say — It was the outcry of a long-felt want [in 1819 Cartwright's petition had a million signers], *a people's protest*. Nothing more or less than that.

when you have consented to the verdict, be not content to note the emptiness of that Chartist hubbub, but take notice also that such outspokenness, albeit over-loud for gentility or discreeter ears, however vainly Jericho-like, was a true and honest and manly utterance, healthier by far than aimless grumbling or the secret conspiracies by Castlereagh's provocation-and-spy system laid grub-like in the hearts of justly discontented Englishmen. Chartism had at least a manlier fibre. Also, underneath and beside all the blatancy were wiser thoughts at work, not able indeed to lead that horn-mad mob in triumph, but even in defeat preparing for future conquest. The better temper of the oppressed, better for all the bellowing, was due to Watson and Hetherington, and their friends, and when the trumpet-braying gave out, some memories of principles taught by them remained. It must also be acknowledged that, although the Charter is not yet law, the very noise scared those in high places, the unhanged Hamans; and poor had been the likelihood of the many changes and many and great improvements in England, in the action of its still usurping legislature and in the condition of its yet unenfranchised people, but for the stirring and striving, so liberally criticized and so satisfactorily condemned, of those insatiable wild beasts, as comfortable reformers suffered them to be called, who only asked for their own rights (for rights not doubted by the men who refused them), who neither harmed nor wished harm to any, and whose worst follies were their being from over-tameness themselves so easily dismayed and sometimes a blind rush, haply incited for their own political ends by the party that drove back and scourged them. To my lords Melbourne, Grey, and Russell, to such well-placed patriots as Brougham, to Burdett and

Hume and O'Connell, be awarded the juster condemna-
tion of History, — for that, having betrayed the people,
they stung them designedly to madness, for the sake of
their own iniquities frustrating the hopes their own pro-
mises had evoked.   No fouler blot smirches our English
record than the conduct of the Great Whig Party from
1830 to 1850 : their treachery toward Freedom culmina-
ting in the acceptance of the Napoleon-Infamy. On the
tomb of the Whigs one word is epitaph : the name of a
trickster : PALMERSTON.   And unless the Miltonic day
must be excepted, the glorious hours of Eliot, Cromwell
and Vane, no worthier cause has occupied the heart of
England in any time than that so unsuccessful struggle
for a "man-like place," the real and avowed object of
the framers of the PEOPLE'S CHARTER.

I am losing sight of Watson, as he, and Hetherington
too, was lost sight of in the whirl of the O'Connor madness.   The demagogues led the multitude by the ears,
while the tyrants looked on, grinning at the confusion,
nor failed to stir the witch-broth when it seemed to cool.
The old plan of inciting in order to betray, rife in those
horrible days of Castlereagh and Sidmouth, and not forgotten during the battle of the Unstamped, [sturdy old
Cobbett made the House of Commons see it when their
own Committee of Inquiry gazed through parliamentary
spectacles in vain], was not left out of the tactics of our
Whigs succeeding to Tory place and practice, although
lack of practice caused their sometimes untoward blun-
dering : blunders of less consequence when every man
to cook "his own goose" and "the land to be bought up
at £40 for an acre" were the cries of the popular wool
gatherers ; and the fleeces followed.

When O'Connor first and afterwards Ernest Jones led

their followers into that wilderness of land-schemes, and the mill-owners, Cobden, Bright, & Co., sought to bribe the ill-fed masses with repeal of the tax on bread (free trade was what they talked about — intending nothing of the sort), wanting cheap bread — the cheapest possible, that "our mills" might be run at less cost and poor-rates reduced to a minimum — [I except those nearer angelic or poetic "free-traders" ignorant of policies and earthly realities, who were persuaded philanthropically to abet any belly-filling schemes, good for at least an afternoon] — Hetherington and Watson stood aside : not denying, but even as strenuously affirming the usurpation of the People's Land, nor heedless of the agony of the hungry poor ; but resolute in their wise perception and determination that before all things it is necessary for a man to be a man, so recognized by the Law and by the custom of Society ; after which he may be strong enough to vindicate other rights. Never before : though the aforesaid poets and good-meaning angels sit in Parliament cheek by jowl with the wealthiest free traders and are regularly allowed to speak, and to vote — in the minority.

Feargus O'Connor and his minions [I believe in the honest intentions of O'Connor, I think a truer man than O'Connell, though of the same not-small-potato breed] never faced the real Chartists — Hetherington, Watson, Lovett ; while in Finsbury, the most radical of metropolitan boroughs, where Moore and Watson lived, represented by surgeon Wakley, stalwart editor of the *Lancet*, and Thomas Slingsby Duncombe,* the Corn-law League

---

* The pluckiest on the Opposition bench : an aristocrat by nature as well as circumstance, yet ever on the people's side, as fearless as Roebuck and more popular, as Roebuck sided with the Whigs in their poor-law policy : a man to be honoured if only for his chivalrous conduct in the exposure

dared not call a public meeting.   Not that an opposing
hand would have been raised in favour of the bread-tax,
but that as from one voice they would have heard the
rebuke of their more selfish policy— Give us our place
of manhood, and that with other injustices shall cease ;
but manhood even before bread !

In the last attempt to inspire the Chartist body with a
reasonable soul Watson stood first.   One of the callers,
and chairman, of the first meeting for congratulation of
the French Republicans on their triumph, in February,
'48, he sought at once to reinvigorate Chartism, toward
a republican party in England.*   But the effort was too
late.   Habits of occasional enthusiasm and evaporation
in blustering talk unfit the best-intentioned for sacrifice
or work, and the earnest man had poor following.   Five
men such as Watson had been powerless for the revival
of Chartism, self-slain.

-----

of the infamous meddling with the Exiles' letters (Mazzini's and others')
in 1844, in the English Post-Office, when the Bandieras were betrayed to
Austria, and Sir James Graham as whipping-boy for Lord Aberdeen got
more than his share of the well-merited but insufficient punishment that
followed that most rascaly un-English proceeding.   My own and Lovett's
letters to Mazzini were among those opened.   He and Watson were of the
few public-spirited enough to characterize the conduct of the Government
as it deserved.   In the Commons' debate Shiel, Macaulay, and Wakley
stood with Duncombe ; but the Liberal Party "would not embarass" the
Ministers.   Even Milner Gibson excused himself from speaking : his head
"too full of Muscovado sugar."   And the Free-Traders, (some excepted,
men such as W. J. Fox, Bridges Adams, old Francis Place, P. A. Taylor,
and W. E. Hickson, editor of the *Westminster Review*), were of course
regardless of English honour.

* At our first meeting he was unanimously chosen president ; but he gave
way to Thomas Cooper (author of the *Purgatory of Suicides*), then just
from prison, whose name he thought might be more useful.

I first became acquainted with Watson in, I think, 1835. I had been brought up more piously than the Church of England usually requires; but the liberal tendencies of my brother-in-law, Thomas Wade, the poet (then editor of *Bell's New Weekly Messenger*, a semi-radical London newspaper), some reading of Voltaire and Shelley, and the stirring words of Lamennais in his famous Scripture anathematized by the Pope *— the *Paroles d'un Croyant*, had brought me in contact with the religious and social and political problems of the time. More especially I was indebted, through occasional attendance at his lectures, to William Johnson Fox, the sometime Unitarian minister, the most eloquent orator of his day, the virtual founder of that new school of English radicalism, which looked beyond the established traditions of the French Revolution, and, more poetical, escaped the narrowness of Utilitarianism: a man wiser than his compeers, who but for lack of boldness (perhaps accounted for by his physique) had been the royal leader of the English democracy. So prepared I was ready for active sympathy with the cause of the people, then finding expression in the cry for political enfranchisement. Almost every day I passed a certain book-shop, a few doors from Bunhill Fields [the Dissenters' burial-ground: John Bunyan lay there,— but there was a talk lately of building over it]; and often I stopped to buy one of Roebuck's *Pamphlets*

---

* "We damn for ever this book of small size but huge depravity."
                                                    Pope Gregory XVI.

or Gilbert A'Becket's *Figaro in London* (the forerunner
of *Punch*), Volney's *Ruins of Empires*, the *Lectures on
History*, or such-like : sometimes remaining to talk with
the shopkeeper, a thin, haggard, thoughtful man, with a
grave yet gentle manner, who appeared more interested
than tradesmen usually are in the worth of what he sold.
This was Watson, recently from prison, and still suffering the effects of his imprisonment.

In 1838 I was projecting what I hoped might become
a sort of cheap library for the people : to consist mainly
of selected extracts from such prohibited works as were
beyond the purchasing-reach or time for study of working men ; and I had grown into so much confidence in
Watson that I went to him to publish for me.   He laid
before me the difficulties in my way, the cost of money
and of obloquy ; then, finding me still resolute, offered
to me (a nameless stranger) his books and his services.
At the end of six months, a volume of weekly numbers
completed, my means nearly used up, I reckoned with
him.   The account rendered, I notice   ~e was
no charge for folding or stitching — some two .   sand
a week — say fifty thousand sheets in all.   He had been
"sure that the book could not pay," and he and his wife
had folded and stitched every copy, to save me so much
of expense.

So began our friendship,— a friendship for which, as
for other such, I paid with the loss of early friends and
home affections : for in those days (not fifty years ago)
Deists were certainly Atheists ; Unitarians were not allowed to call themselves Christians ; and a good church
man of the established persuasion would disown his son
and the mother pass him in the street, unspoken to, for
no better reason than that he refused to join publicly in

their communion,— not from preference for any vicious pleasures (which would have been forgiven), but only because of consciencious scruples, inoffensively avowed, which rendered him liable to the name of Infidel.   The man so treated was my friend.   I speak of what I know. For Unitarians, they lived, married, and traded, among themselves : a proscribed class, though the worthiest of England's sons and daughters, and the foremost English thinkers, were of that sect.   The friendship of one such as Watson was cheaply bought at the price.

For years after, working in the same cause, our course of public action one, our trust in each other unlimited, I familiar in his home and he always welcomed in mine, we moved together in every endeavour of the time : his earlier friend Hetherington not closer to him, I believe, than I was.   So I learned to know him thoroughly.   If I speak here of myself, it is to warrant my speaking of him ; and I have a right to the honour his comradeship bestows upon me.

When Frost and his fellow rebels, Zephaniah Williams and Jones, were condemned to death as leaders in that mad outbreak at Newport brought about by the foolish bluster of O'Connor, it was in the little sitting-room be-hind Watson's shop that we copied out the petition for a reprieve, the subscriptions to which, in not many hours, became so numerous that the Government was fain, for all reluctance, to send a stay of the death-sentence (the punishment was afterwards commuted to transportation for life) to Hetherington's more prominent place of bu-siness, in the Strand, to be there exhibited in order to allay the popular excitement.

Later, in 1840 or '41, when the Government visited its political opponents, the working-class, with indictments for blasphemy, (the pretext a mere sale, amongst other publications, of an intemperate book, Haslam's *Letters to the Clergy*, so pushed into notoriety), and Heywood, one of the prosecuted, advised retaliation upon Government partisans, that goose and gander might be served with the same sauce, it was Watson, with Hetherington, who took up the case in London, by indicting four metropolitan booksellers of unimpeachable respectability for the same offence of blasphemy, — inasmuch as they had published or exposed for sale the "blasphemous and seditious" works of one Percy Bysshe Shelley, containing notably his *Queen Mab*, for which already, indeed many years before, William Clark (if I mistake not the name) had incurred the vengeance of offended Law. We knew of course that the book would but sell the more for prosecution ; we had no desire that it should be otherwise : but if social disgrace from a conviction for "blasphemy" was to be used as a weapon against us, it seemed politic that, boomerang-like, it should return on its employers. Conviction was sure : Law, like Physic, always obedient to Precedent. Our purpose was to prevent the trial of Hetherington,* or to affect his sentence, if condemned. The first object was defeated : the indicted parties getting their trials removed from the Old-Bailey sessions to the higher Court of Queen's Bench, and delaying them by buying off our indispensable witness to the purchase of the books, a compositor in Hetherington's employ, a former apprentice of his. And here occurred two incidents which may give some insight into the character of these men, stigmatized as seditious and as stirrers up of

---

* Cleave also had been indicted, but the indictment was withdrawn on his promise to sell no more. The others were not men to compromise.

strife, etc., as of old, it is said, were certain other men, not altogether unlike these, in Athens and Ephesus and elsewhere.   Hetherington had determined not to pay a fine.   "They might take it out of his bones :" if not so courtly in expression, yet of the same courage as brave Sir John Eliot's answer to Charles I.   And this martyr also had his possessions : a shop and books, presses and other printing-material, besides household-stuff.   Once before all had been swept off ; he would be wiser now. Two or three days before the trial I was with him when he called upon the London ·agent of an old good friend, Hugh Williams, a Caermarthen lawyer.*   Williams had ordered for a sufficient sum to be paid to Hetherington, who passed the same to the hand of one of his shopmen named Powell.†   He thereupon bought of Hetherington his whole property, brokers being called in to value all, in order to legalize the sale ; and Hetherington, return- ing his friend's loan, went penniless into Court, to meet the most that could be inflicted.   He defended himself ‡ with much eloquence and moderation, in spite of a very

* In after days the instigator and undiscovered leader of the one suc- cessful uprising in Britain since Cromwell,— the "Rebecca" movement in South Wales : a movement intended by him to be *educational*.   His sister, a woman of decided character and, I believe, of republican prin- ciples, was the wife of Richard Cobden.

† THOMAS POWELL (so trusted and in that and all other respects most worthy of trust — I need hardly say that he handed back the property to his friend) was a Chartist like the rest of us.   He too had had his twelvemonths gaol-lesson, graduating in patriotism.   Caught for some unguarded words, which were wrested into illegal contrary meanings, he was punished for being strong enough to hold men back, a man more dangerous than the mere mob-inciter.   After the failure of Chartism he busied himself with organizing an emigration party, to South America. That too failed.   He died, a few years later, in Trinidad.

‡ The Defence he dedicated to Watson.

bitter and unfairly personal attack of Attorney-General
Campbell; was complimented for it by Denman, then
Chief-Justice; and sentenced to the lightest punishment
upon record — imprisonment for six weeks in a debtors'
prison. When he came out we were still looking for his
compositor. One day walking together, Hetherington
and Watson accidentally met the man; and their moral
influence was sufficient to outweigh the bribe which had
first tempted him. He came into Court, gave evidence,
and Moxon, notwithstanding the eloquent pleading of
Talfourd, was found guilty. It remained for the prose-
cutors to call him up for judgment, which of course was
never done, personal animosity or revenge being beside
the question; nor was further proceeding taken against
the other indicted "blasphemers," Frazer, Richardson,
and Saunders of the firm of Saunders and Ottley. We
had gained enough. Prosecutions for blasphemy were
estopped. I think there has since been only one, with
foolish wilfulness provoked, for the sake of a spurious
notoriety.

In the matter of these prosecutions, as in all other in
which I had occasion to act with him, Watson's conduct
commanded general respect; he knew nor undue haste
nor wavering, but walked straight toward his aim as one
whose will went forth to conquer; his judgment never
was at fault. But for his modesty, he had all the qualities of a leader. Yet, ever unobtrusive and unassuming
as he was, he led, in virtue of his quiet self-possession,
his sterling good sense, his dauntless courage, and that
unbounded trust which all his associates placed in him.
When the dispute was at its highest between "physical"
and "moral," force to the needless disintegration of the
Chartist body,— when the old steadily earnest party of

Lovett and Hetherington and Watson was outvoiced by
the O'Connorites, and impulsive Hetherington came in
for his share of objurgation and abuse, never was there
an ill word or disrespectful spoken against Watson. His
calm and dignified bearing, his justice toward all men,
his well-considered language even when most indignant,
lifted him above the reach of calumny or the intemper-
ance of anger, however unsparing the severity of his rebuke — never unfairly personal — when severity became
a public duty. Strongly, sternly opposed to the empty
braggart speech and conduct in which our hopes of universal suffrage were wrecked, when active patriotism at
last meaned only a mad mob howling to the praise and
glory of Feargus O'Connor and Ernest Jones (but demagogues however well-desiring) and G. W. M. Reynolds,
the tin kettle at the mad mob's tail,— I think there was
not one of his opponents who would have done him any
harm, who did not honour him even when most hostile.
And his friends, beyond the closer circle of his fellow-
workers :— his friends were Mazzini, and Mazzini's old
comrade and dearest of all friends, the more than noble
Pole, Stanislaus Worcell, by birth a noble, yet nobler in
exile-martyrdom ; and William Bridges Adams, rail-way
engineer, a man as magnificently disinterested as James
Watson himself ; and Francis Sibson, physician, brother
of the artist ;. and the present Member for Newcastle on
Tyne, Joseph Cowen ; and —— Surely these witnesses
to character are sufficient : else I could cite many more,
dead and living, lovers and admirers of his worth.

Some were in strong sympathy with his principles and
so perhaps prepossessed in his favour ; others, misliking
his surroundings or without care for his mode of action,
no less esteemed the man : he had no lack of friendship

beyond the range of his political or religious walk. Nor
was he himself so narrow that he could not work except
for his special life-purpose : not to the direct hindrance
of that. Though he held to the Charter as the one and
most urgent need of the time, and refused to accept the
Reform Bill as payment of the People's Debt or peddle
the People's birthright for any mess of corn-law pottage,
he worked zealously for the few honest men in the Whig
House of Commons, none more actively for Duncombe
and Wakley, by the exertions of him and Moore and of
others of the same Chartist faction repeatedly returned
to Parliament for the borough of Finsbury. Mazzini's
" People's International League "* had his prompt adhe-
sion, his constant attention, and his ready subscription
to the full reach of his scanty means. Of foreign affairs
he cared to be informed; and the exiles, Italian, Polish,
and French, found in him an unfalteringly loyal friend.
His sympathies, as his principles, were sure, both firmly
based ; and wide. He was great-hearted, and fearless.
Despising bluster, and disliking force, if force might be
avoided,— a peaceable man, but not for peace at whatever price,— he could not keep silence when the men of
Bradford were insurgent, but while the politic hesitated
boldly defended their right to judge for themselves how

---

* Formed in 1847, at the instigation and with the help of Mazzini, in
· · r "To enlighten the British Public as to the political condition and
relations of Foreign Countries ; to disseminate the principles of National
Freedom and Progress; to embody and manifest an efficient public op-
nion in favour of the right of every People to Self-government and the
maintenance of their own Nationality ; and to promote a good under-
standing between the Peoples of all Countries." On the list of Council
stood the names of W. B. Adams, Dr. Bowring, W. J. Fox, Goodwyn
Barmby, Douglas Jerrold, T. S. Duncombe, P. A. Taylor, P. A. Taylor
junior, beside others: the last-named, both father and son, with Moore
and Watson, of the Council also, the most active of its members.

soon the time of patience was over and the occasion for
resistance come.   He was, as I have already said, one
of the conveners of the first public meeting in England
to congratulate the French on their Revolution of 1848;
he was on the Committee to help the latest Polish insur-
rection, in 1863—4.   Latest, not last.

His own account has told us, only too briefly, of the
Fast-day in 1832 : when, the country being afflicted with
cholera, an enlightened Government on the prescription
of a certain Saint Percival, not a doctor of medicine, ordered its removal (the removal of the cholera) by exhi-
bition of one day's general fast and solemn performance
of prayer to Almighty God. Performance, going through
a form, says Ruskin.   Orthodox salt-cod-and-egg-sauce
in respectable society — I need not pause to enumerate
the necessary accompanying wines, condiments, etc., —
seeming to the radical and perhaps impious Association
of working-men no specific for an evil starvation-helped
(with fifteen hundred persons in one London poorhouse
— eight and ten to a bed, "from the putrid and noxious
atmosphere dying off like rotten sheep,"), these radical
and so impracticable working-men refused obedience to
the ministerial edict ; and forbidden to work on the law-
appointed holiday, nor allowed (under old ecclesiastical
law revived for the occasion) to hold a public meeting,
thought therefore to protest in such manner as was left
to them,— to show by a quiet procession how many dis-
approved of Percivalism — State-humbug, and after the
walk to provide a dinner for the poorer members of the
Association.   But the police obstructed and dispersed
them ; and afterwards arrested the prime movers of the
procession, Watson, Lovett, and Benbow, and had them
brought to trial at the next sessions for intention to riot

and breach of the peace. Of course no one supposed it
was so. The object of the prosecution was to damage
the National Union through its leaders. Twelve men,
from the people, not specially selected, are not often on
the side of any tyranny in England. These, as the jury
in the Calthorpe Street affair, and later in the matter of
the *Poor Man's Guardian*, gave their deliberate verdict
for the public liberties : a verdict of *Not Guilty*, after a
spirited speech from each of the accused, Watson's very
manly and straightforward, principally in vindication of
the public right, at the same time insisting on their own
peaceful conduct.

One of many witnesses voluntarily appearing to prove
the peaceable, orderly behaviour of the procession was
a member of the Common Council of London, Richard
Taylor, a master-printer, a man of liberal views but not
active in politics, highly esteemed in the City, of some
note for editing Horne Tooke's *Diversions of Purley*.

On a later occasion for protesting (in 1846, I think),
another Fast-day, this time for relief of Irish famine, we
had our public meeting, Watson in the chair, and from
among the audience rose old Richard Taylor, to remind
his friend the chairman of that former day, to congratulate him on the greater freedom we had gained, ending
his unexpected speech with warm praise of him for his
persistent endeavouring and for the blameless character
he had maintained throughout his course.

Persistence in all that he considered right and careful
avoidance of any just cause for blame were indeed cha-
racteristics of the man.

Let us look back to the prison history! In September, 1822, Watson came up to London, and spent Christmas with Carlile in jail, as foretaste of the course of instruction preparing for him in that Liberal University. Six weeks of real imprisonment before trial in the beginning of the next year, and then he remains for the full term of twelve months. Time for mature consideration out of which to shape his future life. That twelve months imprisonment was not lost upon him.

Of that year in Cold-Bath-Fields prison I have some record in his own words. He was not ill-treated by his keepers; he had a room to himself; his friends were allowed to visit him at certain times; even the Governor would drop in upon him for a talk; he read much, and made notes of what he read; used his "opportunity for study and investigation;" kept also some sort of diary, I fancy even more monotonous than diaries usually are. Here, however, are two entries that will interest us.

April 21, 1824—

"This day the Governor visited me. I had some of my lumber removed from the prison, as a prelude to self removal, and am not sorrowful for the circumstance. I wrote letters to friends Byerley and Driver of Leeds and received a letter from Mr. Carlile. The weather warm and calm."

April 22—

"This day I had all my chattels removed from the prison, except my box. Had a long walk with Mrs. Wright

[the wife of a Leeds bookseller ; in prison for the same offence as Watson, for selling in Carlile's shop] ; drank a couple of glasses of rum-punch with my fellow-prisoners, Mr. Humphreys and Mr. Lord [no political sinners, one for smuggling tobacco] ; the Governor [evidently impressed in his favour] congratulated me on the near termination of my imprisonment. The weather fine and warm."

Fine warm Spring weather : who does not understand the freed prisoner's gladness, and the joy of that home visit to the good, anxious mother, "to convince her that imprisonment had not made him a worse son." A good son surely, as sure to be a worthy citizen ! Now back to London for a livelihood, in order to fulfil the duties of a citizen. But already he is a marked man : who will employ one of Carlile's shopmen ? Let him seek work and not find and, wanting bread, learn the worst misery of the proscribed ! He is young. Fortunately Carlile still needs him, will have him to conduct his business.

Perhaps this position as manager, and afterwards his employment as compositor on the *Republican*, saved him from another imprisonment : the governmental raid was upon those who *sold* the publications. Then came that kindly fever which took him to the care of good Julian Hibbert, procuring for him his noble friendship, finding him work until the Spring of 1828.

He was not abandoning the cause for which he had at first adventured. The man was unchangeable. Though somewhile brought up under the shadow of a shovel-hat, he had with him his mother : a woman who would read Cobbett's "*Gridiron*" even in a parsonage. And his first experience of punishment only set him more resolutely on the way he had traced out for himself, for the public good. He came to London, an unknown man, in 1822. In 1828 we find him acting as store-keeper of the "First London Co-operative Trading Association," in Red-Lion Square, Holborn : in the formation of which association and others similar * he had been an active helper.

In the following year he took the management of another store, in Jerusalem Passage, Clerkenwell. In '30 he rented a house, in Windmill Street, letting the upper part, and retaining for his own uses only two rooms on the ground-floor. The front room was his shop, with a deal table for counter, on which to place his papers and books : no trashy "light" literature among them. The back room was his home : an old sofa did duty for bed ; he was his own servant for all work, preparing his own spare meals, waiting upon himself. And here he began to print for his own publications, when customers were not, or working before and after the hours of business. Lowell's words on Garrison may be applied to him :—

> "In a small chamber, friendless, and unseen,
>   Toil'd o'er his types one poor, unlearn'd young man ;
> The place was dark, unfurnitured and mean ;—
>   Yet there the freedom of a race began.

> " Help came but slowly ; surely no man yet
>   Put lever to the heavy world with less :
> What need of help ? He knew how types were set ;
>   He had a dauntless spirit, and a press. "

---

* The fore-runners of the more successful co-operative stores of to-day. The first of these associations was, I believe, started at Brighton, in 1828 ; and numerous others soon followed throughout the country : the first necessary funds raised by weekly contributions of all the members. They failed, after many trials, perhaps from many causes : one sufficient, that there was then no legal security for such associations,— association for any purpose whatever discountenanced by the ruling powers.

After a while he so far enlarged his domain as to make room for a housekeeper, his niece, his sister's daughter, afterwards the wife of his friend Richard Moore.

The Fast-day prosecution was in 1832, when the jury stood between him and a second imprisonment: counting preliminary six weeks in 1823 as nothing. In '33 he was with his friend and fellow-offender Hetherington in Clerkenwell prison: six months each for the *Poor Man's Guardian*. This, what we call his second prison-service, had such aggravation of punishment as is disclosed by his Petition to the "Commons;" the deprivation of that which is most cared for by decent men: some privacy, some mental solace and respectable society. Subjected to the companionship of the vilest and most brutal criminals, a compelled listener to "the most horrid swearing and the grossest licentiousness;" refused even occasional withdrawal to the retirement of a solitary cell — [a separate sleeping-cell, which had not been obtained without urgent solicitation. If I mistake not, both he and Hetherington had at the first to sleep in the general ward.]: and this suffering, this moral torture, dread of vermin and disease superadded, was inflicted on them illegally, under the summary jurisdiction of police-magistrates, for selling a paper which afterwards, upon trial before a Jury, was declared to be a publication strictly according to Law.

That six months passed; and he was not crushed, nor converted. Only with Hibbert's legacy he began to enlarge his publishing operations, and continued active as ever in political and co-operative movements.

In 1834 he moved to 18, Commercial-place, City-road — still Finsbury: being one of the lessees and manager of the Hall of Science, a hall near by, used for popular

meetings ; having care of that as well as his own trade.
Here, having now thirty-five years of age, he on the 3d
of June brought home a Wife, the daughter of his old
(somewhile deceased) friend Robert Byerley.

Now surely he will give up a single man's enthusiasm,
and provide first hereafter for the interests of his family
and home.   He is of more heroic mould.   Duty to him
is (not independent of, but) higher than wife or home.
And his wife is one with him : would not seduce him to
play the craven.   She has married him to be his helper,
not his hinderer.   On the 3d of June he is married ; a
week later he goes with his wife, to see his old bed-rid
mother, eighty-two years of age, and before the end of
the month is again summoned as an offender to the po-
lice-court.   On the 7th of August he again enters his
prison, for six months more, leaving the newly-wedded
wife to manage his business during his absence.   I give
in her own words what here follows.

"We were married on the 3d of June, 1834.   On the
25th he was sentenced (in his absence) for selling the
Conservative, one of Hetherington's unstamped papers.
He left home ; stayed a day or two with Hetherington ;
wrote me directions about the business, of which I then
knew nothing ; and then went to Jersey, to the house of
his first London friend, Thomas Hooper.*   He returned
in August, and was with me for a few days.   On the 7th
of August two Bow-street officers arrested him : he was
going along the City-road [on some election business].
They let him return a moment, to bid me farewell : and
then took him to Clerkenwell Prison.   I went every day

---

* A right worthy friend ! Of whom Mrs. Watson adds, writing to me
since her husband's death, — "A true, kind friend to me now ; proud
of their fifty years friendship."

but two (Sundays excepted) all the six months. It was
a bitter winter; but we never met under a roof, only in
the open yard, with no seat. They let me take him food
and sheets for his loose straw bed, which was on a shelf,
in a bare stone cell ;— no fire ;— no glass, but only bars
to the windows.   Some books I took him (Lawrence's
Lectures on Physiology, Morgan's *Philosophy of Morals*,)
they would not allow him to have."

In his prison he writes to cheer the young wife : one
day, perhaps, when she can not come : a letter that may
give some glimpses of the man's nature.

"New Prison, Clerkenwell : September 12, 1834.
"My dearest Ellen ! I read and re-read your note.   .
Do not suppose that my imprisonment gives me pain : it
is not that ; it is the separation from you.   .   Never
mind ! I am now recovering, and your love and attach-
ment will more than repay all I have endured.   I have
no wish beyond that of making you happy and endeavouring as far as possible to make the world, or rather its
inhabitants, more comfortable.   I want neither wealth
nor greatness. Your confidence and the means honestly
to pay my way are the bounds of my ambition.   I care
not how much I have to work, nor for the quality or the
quantity of the food I eat, so long as I can keep clear
of dependence upon others. Surely we can do this.   .

"I am fond of home, of privacy, of books, of a select
society of friends.   .   .   .   .

"Do not let my staidness disconcert you or make you
think I am unhappy. Remember, my dear Ellen ! what
a school of adversity I have been trained in, the obstacles I have had to encounter, the struggles I have had
to make ; to which add that my studies, by choice — I
admit, have been of a painful kind.   The study of the

cause and remedy for human woe has engrossed all my thoughts.   .   .   .   .

"No one has stronger attachments when once formed,
    .   .   my Mother is to me an everlasting affection. She deserves it too : yet I never could pen those empty and heartless words that some can."

Truly a man not given to express his feelings in many words.   A man of the puritan, or quaker stamp : silent and reserved save when occasion called him out.   Then he was a ready and impressive speaker, if not eloquent. But if his tenderest heart-thoughts had not words, they had the richer growth of deeds.   His loving kindnesses toward his mother and sister,* toward all his relations, and his wife's also, so far as his means enabled were generously manifested.— I turn back to his letters.   Here is his prison life :—

"I bear my position cheerfully.   See how I pass my time.   I rise between eight and nine ; wash and shave ; breakfast, wash up my cup and saucer ; walk for a time ; sit down ; read some instructive or amusing book ; then pass a delightful hour with you ; walk again ; dine, and read ; walk again ; tea ; walk a short time.   Locked up in my dormitory, five feet wide by seven feet long, make my straw bed ; sit down and read or write [There was no fire in his cell, those winter nights.] until eleven or

---

* Fifteen years older than himself.   "A gentle, loving creature, very proud of her brother :" says the wife, writing to me lately.

By her work as a dress-maker she helped her mother to support him during his childhood.   She afterwards married a carpenter, on whose earnings of fifteen shillings a week, supplemented by her own, she had to bring up, and brought up well, a large family.   In those expressive words of Ebenezer Elliott, a many-childed, bone-weary woman ; a quiet quaker-like gentlewoman, as I remember her, of nice manners, worthy of any position, of any companionship or surroundings.

twelve o'clock; then think of you as I lay down for the night. Thus I pass my time. Were you with me, what would signify bolts, bars, or locks? Take care of yourself! You are to me everything."

From other letters — as manly, as affectionate, as uncomplaining, bearing witness to the bravery and gentle-heartedness of the man as well as to the worth and fortitude of the wife, I could but will not quote. So much given may be sufficient, from letters not meaned for any eyes but those of the loved and loving.

Now again be repeated those Words of a Believer :—
When you see a man led to prison, or punishment, say not in your haste — This is some wicked man who has committed a crime against his fellows!
For peradventure it is a good man —
Nay! not per adventure : through any chance or happening. This *surely is* the good man who has striven to serve his fellows, and so is punished by the oppressors.

Well, having fulfilled this third term, six months for illegal selling of the *Conservative*, he came out of prison on the twenty-first of January, 1835. Be it noted that the *Guardian*, between which and the *Conservative* there was scarcely a technical difference, had been declared a strictly legal publication in June of the preceding year. But both papers were Hetherington's, and by aid of the technicality the authorities had their way. After this Watson was unmolested. Indeed by Hetherington and him and their five or six hundred assistants the Government had been defeated.

My story has been of public life and acts, with only such glimpses of the man himself as could not but appear in that relation. What presentment have I given of him? Chiefly of a stern, uncompromising antagonist, a stiffly upright stirrer of strife, hard, obstinate, and rebellious? His enemies might have seen him in this light: his only enemies the wrong-doers against whom he stood. And my readers, some perchance, may not have seen further. A plain working-man, habited, even as he was fed and lodged, no better than an ordinary mechanic, who held mere finery in contempt, who would have no luxuries of any kind, who had been ashamed of the appearance of costliness or indulgence while men hungered within his reach; a rigid puritan, whose eyes were sad, whose aspect was severe, who had nor quips nor cranks for your amusement:— Does this describe him? His photograph without name beneath it would pass for portrait of one of Cromwell's Ironsides. I know no modern face with more of that seventeenth-century religiously earnest character. But look at it again! Those sad eyes under the bent brows are full of womanly tenderness. A smile of kindliest benevolence, ay! and a sense of humour too, lurks around the firm-set lips. This man, who had not shrunk from any martyrdom,— I have seen him fling his hat over his head and leap up as he had in his boyhood, according to an old country superstition, when he heard the cuckoo for the first time in Spring. This man, the firm voice of whose severity rebuked throned Injustice,

E

drew the little children to his knees by the undoubted gentleness of his inviting glance. If he had not much fun, no word a girl should not have heard was ever on his tongue; his manner, though grave, was cheerful; if self-possessed and strict, he was yet companionable; patient with opposition; never querulous; considerate for others in all respects; stoutly set upon his own way, but tolerant of those who went differently; not harsh, albeit hard against tyranny and vice. Vice of himself he knew not. If ever there was a virtuous man, it was he. His moral conduct was irreproachable. The white marble statue, which his life deserved, was not more pure, more free from flaw or stain. And let it be remarked that his youth was in the days of George, Prince-regent, (the sty time of England) when even the "goddess" Liberty, so lately come from France, had something of the harlot in her nature; when men in their extreme reaction against repression forgot the righteousness of self-restraint, and freedom for the sake of Order, the freedom of the stars in their appointed courses, seemed almost hypocrisy or was dreaded to be a new phase of the old Unequal Law. The wandering, the excesses, the licenciousness of even noble men of that day would have more excuse if their judges (of this present generation) could realize their surroundings, and recall the intoxication of that time of renewed youth to Western Europe, in which the double chain of monarchy and priestcraft was riven by France, —though soldered since, no more to be reforged. Days of the Saturnalia of freed slaves! The chains but now knocked off, the walk is not that of sober freemen. To return to one for whom excuse was never needed.

Severe and self-denying as Watson was, he was warm of heart, and generous to the full extent of his means.

Devoting all his gains to further public services, he had little respite from his work. His one holiday, for sake of health, was an occasional day or, when it could be so managed, some days in the country (for which he born and bred there naturally yearned), and long rambles in the fresh air with some friend. Many an hour have we spent together under the trees of Woodford forest, within one day's easy reach of London; and no artist companion I ever had more thoroughly enjoyed the scenery and the mountain-climbs in our beautiful Lake Country than did Watson when, after a severe sickness, he came to recruit with me then living at Brantwood (the home now of Ruskin), by Coniston-Water. Seriously then we talked of his coming, whenever he could withdraw from business, to live with me and help in my republican propagandism and the bringing out of my *English Republic.* After circumstances, not the will of either, hindered the fulfilment of our purpose, to my loss.

I have said, the country holidays were his one enjoyment, his one recreation and rest. Not that he had not other tastes; but he spared neither time nor money for his pleasures. But after he gave up publishing he took a lodging for himself and wife in the neighbourhood of the Crystal Palace, at Norwood, so that he might daily wander among its treasures of art and manufacture and hear the music. I go back to earlier times.

Three years, including the prison time, he rented the house in Commercial-place; then for a year he found it more convenient to occupy the lower rooms of the Hall of Science. From there he removed across the street to 15 City-road. In 1843 he had a shop at 5 Paul's Alley, and afterwards at 3 Queen's Head Passage, Paternoster Row, where I find him some eleven years later, the date

of the testimonial.   The upper part of the house in the
Passage he had however let, retaining only the shop for
his own use; and had for some two or three years been
living, in easier circumstances but simply as of old, at
17 Thornhill Terrace (127 Hemingford-road), Islington.
Here he continued to reside until, I think, 1865 or '66,
when he went to Norwood, to be within walking reach
of the Crystal Palace.   Though out of business he still
retained his interest in the old questions of freedom of
opinion; and if as years passed by they found him less
active than heretofore, the cause lay in the years themselves, the stagnant years that succeeded a period of so
great excitement.   There was no let or deadening of his
patriotic and philanthropic zeal; the man was yet ready
if opportunity had invited or occasion called him forth.
He aided his friend Moore, throughout the prolonged
struggle for an absolutely untaxed Press; * and was, as
said before, one of the Committee of sympathizers with
unhappy Poland in 1864.   His devoted love of Liberty,
the Liberty which is the right of growth, knew no abate-
ment; and the old man, nearing the term of three-score
and ten years, was young at heart.

The evening of his life was worthy of the morning.
Happy in his home with a wife who loved and honoured
him; loved and honoured too by many friends; in fair
health (though tried in earlier years); with an income
(not greater indeed than a day-labourer's) sufficient for

---

* Some idea may be had of the labour here involved when I state, on
Collet's authority, that the Committee of which Moore was chairman
[appointed by the People's Charter Union as the "Newspaper (*penny*)
Stamp Abolition Committee," afterwards Committee of the Association
for repeal of all the taxes on knowledge,] from its formation, in 1849,
to the abolition of the duty on paper, in 1861, had to meet 473 times.

his simple needs and all his own earning, his books and leisure, and outside opportunities of enjoyment: he had the well-deserved reward of all his consciencious work, his self-denial and devotedness for the good of others. Day by day there was his walk to the Palace, and hours of quiet pleasure, viewing and examining the marvels of art and science there stored. More than all, there was a never-failing delight in the frequent concerts. Knowing not a note of music, he yet had a liking for the best. He would come home and say—"I am late, but we had a selection from Handel (or from Mozart or Beethoven) on the Grand Organ, and I could not but stay to hear it." Sometimes the wife accompanied him. Often too he would meet old friends,— it might be by accident, it might be they had come with purpose to see and spend some hours with him. But he was no less happy alone. So passed the next five or six years.

A severe sickness of his wife, in 1872, first broke him down. Fear for her, anxiety and exertion, over-taxed his strength. When, returning from America, I last saw him, in 1872–3, he was suffering from intensest melancholy without apparent cause, and failing fast. Winter of 1873–4 he stayed at Blaydon-on-Tyne, at the house of Joseph Cowen, who, and his wife also, esteemed and loved him; and their careful kindness seemed to revive him. Helped further by a journey into Wales with his old friend Hooper, he rallied for a while. It was only for a while. The sadness returned. Still he would go to the Palace: the music cheered him. But the fire of life was flickering out. Some days of wavering memory, one week in bed,— and the weary had found his rest: passing away in his sleep, without a struggle, without a sigh. He died on the twenty-ninth of November 1874, at Burns Cottage, Hamilton-road, Lower Norwood ; and was buried in Norwood Cemetery.—— A plain granite obelisk erected over the grave, through the ready action of an old Chartist comrade, Joseph A. Corfield, marks the spot where sleeps that "noblest work of God"—

AN HONEST MAN.

On the grey granite obelisk is the following inscription :

JAMES WATSON

1874

ERECTED BY A FEW FRIENDS AS A TOKEN OF REGARD
FOR HIS INTEGRITY OF CHARACTER
AND HIS BRAVE EFFORTS TO SECURE
THE RIGHT OF FREE SPEECH
AND
A FREE AND UNSTAMPED PRESS

And on a square block of polished red granite beneath :

IN MEMORY OF
JAMES WATSON
PUBLISHER

Born Sept. 21, 1799 — died Nov. 29, 1874

Gentle as brave he shunn'd no duteous strife
  To help his fellow men opposing wrong.
Scorning reward, he freely spent his life ;
  And made of all his days a patriot song.

In personal appearance Watson was not remarkable : he would not have been spoken of as handsome, though he was well-made and well-featured, and of goodly stature, —his passport says—"height 5 feet, 8 inches" (I would have said taller), and "light complexion, blue eyes and brown hair;" square-shouldered, and firmly but sparely made, certainly no tendency to corpulence. His head square and well set ; his features regular ; till late in life close-shaven. In the latter years he let his beard grow. In ordinary talk his manner was generally serious, earnest always, his matter weighty and sincere ; the tone of his voice was pleasant, his words were correct and well spoken : sometimes with those nearest to him, or when moved, recurring to the Yorkshire old country form, yet used, the quaker *thou* and *thee*, instead of *you*. On the platform his bearing was simple and dignified, earnest, and impressive, and without gestures ; his speech unhesitating but deliberate, well-chosen words clearly enunciated, and sound argument. No oratorical display, but straight-hitting strong good sense delivered direct from the heart. He seemed always, and in private as well as public, to have before him the ideal of what an English workman ought to be [I think of him always as a workman because, though he had a shop, he was in no sense a tradesman — a buyer and seller for gain], not through any priggish assumption born of introspective formality. Too healthy a man to require continual self-probing, he grew, as a tree, in worthiness, though using his human reason in training and pruning for more certain growth.

Of his political opinions there is little need to speak, after all already told. They may be summed up as of the school of Paine, whose writings have been, and still are, the political Gospel of our English working classes. The more philosophical views of the French revolutionists, whatever additional impulse they have given, were never so well digested by the masses as the plainer common sense of their own countryman. French teachings rather had issue in the thoughts of the more scholarly of English politicians, an indirect rather than a direct influence upon English action.

On his religious meditations I do not care to intrude. Such speculations, so far as they concern only the man himself, it seems to me are no concern of any one else. Had he been questioned, I think he might have replied in the words of Paine — *To do good is my religion ;* and have found sufficient ground for action in these of good old John Woolman — *Whoever rightly advocates the good of some thereby promotes the good of the whole.* I would imagine (I do not recollect to have heard him say) that his faith was much the same as Paine's : a simple belief in some over-ruling Power which leads the harmony of the Universe, — whence he deduced his maxim of duty, toward which he could not but square his life, uncaring for any bribe of "heaven" nor needing to be driven by dread of "hell." I do not know that he troubled himself about particular providences, or essayed to fathom the Infinite, in order to justify the ways of God ; but I do know that he had a clear perception of righteousness and the Higher Law, to which he reverently bowed his life in daily and hourly worship. Of course I am aware that "only this" takes him from the pale of Christianity and relegates him to the glorious company of "Infidels." Which may not matter much. As he cared not to talk of what thoughtful speculations stirred his soul, I shall not pretend to speak concerning them, but rather leave his religion with this report, indefinite or precise according to the reader's judgment. For myself, I learned his faith sufficiently from his work.

His favourite poem was Bryant's *Thanatopsis :* it may be because expressing his own as calm contemplation of death as rest after a well-spent life. To look for glory or reward was not a necessity for one whose work was reward enough. The last books he read were Forster's Lives of *Sir John Eliot* and *Goldsmith* (Goldsmith but a few days before the end): characteristic of himself,— brave and consciencious as the first, and gentle-hearted as the other.

He was not a man of genius ; he did not care to make a name ; he had "no ambition for authorship." Yet he deserved the oaken crown. I never before considered whether he had or had not genius. In the presence of his integrity of life it seems a question altogether unrequired. God forbid that I should depreciate genius ! Assuredly do I recognize in the flashes of a Byron or a Burns the wondrous lightnings of the Eternal. But in the steady life-splendour of one who never faltered, who never swerved from right, whose careful thought was always obeyed by corresponding deeds, whose word was his bond, whose record is without stain, I perceive — if not the exceptional fire of heaven — the clear common day-light, in which the Highest is revealed to us, as by the pillar of flame, to guide or cheer us on our way.

It has been my rare fortune to have as friends and to be intimate with many noble men : the greatest of this age — of the ages, Joseph Mazzini,— the Polish martyr, Worcell,— the Russian patriot, Herzen,— the venerable Lamennais,— William Bridges Adams,— Leigh Hunt,— beside artist comrades close and dear, Thomas Sibson, Edward Wehnert, Alfred Stevens, and some yet living: — but of no man's friendship am I more proud than of the forty years friendship of JAMES WATSON.

With what more words shall I conclude?   I can find none fitter to my own feeling than those I wrote on first hearing of his death: printed in the New-York *Evening Post*, afterwards in England, in the *Newcastle Chronicle*.

> ONCE more the Powers have taken hence
>   Their own.   Why fall our tears?
> Who gave resume!   O vain defence
>   Of slowly fading years!
>
> How many noble Englishmen,
>   Death! hast thou in thy fold:
> Their legends writ with firmest pen
>   On History's tombs of gold.
>
> Yet he, whom thou hast gather'd now,
>   May rank among thy best,
> Though passing with unlaurel'd brow
>   Unnoticed to his rest.
>
> To-day is come and will depart,—
>   To-morrow none will say—
> From English life our truest heart
>   So lately pass'd away.
>
> Only an obscure workman he,
>   Poor, without place or birth:
> Yet born to make his country free
>   By energy of worth.

O peerless Milton! flawless Vane!
　We miss you doubly now, —
Your thought in him lived once again;
　The same undaunted brow

Was his before the front of Power,
　The same unprison'd soul,
The same clear sight beyond the hour
　To see the further goal.

The same integrity of life:
　He gave it without stint;
And loving peace, yet sought the strife
　At Duty's lightest hint.

A man who knew not how to lie —
　He knew not how to fear:
Upright in his firm honesty,
　And loving as sincere.

A patriot, strict to private due;
　Severe, and yet so sweet,
So glad a nature, his smile drew
　The children round his feet.

O poorly rear'd, as lowly born!
　When thy sad eyes are dim
Before the uplifted hand of Scorn,
　Point thou beyond to him.

O Labour's bondslaves, who would claim
　The freeman's fitter place!
Write in your hearts this labourer's name
　Whose life brought labour grace;

Who made his work a poem grand,
　No poet's words more high;
Who dared and suffer'd, to withstand
　Thy spoilers, Industry!

Not asking for himself reward
    Of praise or worldly part:
Still giving, from the exhaustless hoard
    Of his most royal heart.

Brave as the bravest Ironside,
    Yet gentlest of the brave ——
O Friend! like thee to have lived and died
    Were worth a noteless grave.

Knowing the world's forgetfulness of those who have passed out of sight, I did not when writing those lines expect a monument to be raised to him; nor think until asked by Mrs. Watson of writing this Memoir. Would that it more fully represented my love for him; would that it were worthier of the man!

www.ingramcontent.com/pod-product-compliance
Lightning Source LLC
Chambersburg PA
CBHW081519040426
42447CB00013B/3274